# Viking Poetry
# for Heathen Rites

*Drekktu djúpt inn dýra mjöð!*

# Viking Poetry for Heathen Rites

*Asatru Liturgy in Traditional Verse*

## Eirik Westcoat

Skaldic Eagle Press
Long Branch, Pennsylvania
2017

Copyright © 2017 Eirik Westcoat

With proper attribution (for example, verbally or in a program booklet), the poems in this book may be freely read out loud (with or without minor changes) in not-for-profit religious rituals or poetry readings, whether private or public. All other rights reserved.

For permissions or other information, please contact the author at <eirik@theskaldiceagle.com> or <http://www.theskaldiceagle.com/>.

Cover art by Jesseca Trainham
All layout and design by Eirik Westcoat

First Edition, Midsummer 2017

9 8 7 6 5 4 3 2 1

**Casewrap Hardcover ISBN: 978-1-947407-00-8**
Trade Paperback ISBN: 978-1-947407-01-5
PDF Ebook ISBN: 978-1-947407-02-2
EPUB Ebook ISBN: 978-1-947407-03-9
Kindle Ebook ISBN: 978-1-947407-04-6

Skaldic Eagle Press
Long Branch, Pennsylvania

*For the Hearth of Yggdrasil*

# Acknowledgements

The idea for this book was one of the earliest inspirations I received from the Mead of Poetry. It has been a long road to its completion, and many deserve thanks for their active help with it or for contributing to the conditions that allowed it to grow.

First and foremost, my thanks go to the Hearth of Yggdrasil, to whom this book is dedicated. They supported my development as a poet during its earliest days, and many of the poems in this book were first recited in their rituals or other events. The development of a liturgy must have a religious community as its context, and without the Hearth of Yggdrasil, I might not have had that context, and this book would likely have been quite different.

Next, thanks go to the Rune-Gild, that august initiatory school, which enabled me to make the self-transformation necessary to becoming the skald and scholar that I am today, and whose curriculum lead me to encounter the Mead of Poetry. This book comprises the largest part of my Masterwork with them. Great credit also goes to the East Coast Thing, for the spark via a lore contest that got me started on writing poetry in late 2010, and for the reception it has given to my poetry there in the years afterwards, both in its skaldic competition and outside of it.

Thanks also go to Jesseca Trainham for her wonderful cover art and to Laura Kemmerer for copyediting the text and to Scott Mohnkern for further proofreading. Furthermore, I thank my family for supporting my endeavors over the years, but most especially my mother, Janet Westcoat, for support in publishing this book and my brother, Jeffrey "Sigurd" Westcoat, for offering feedback on many of my poems.

Finally, thanks go to the gods, the Aesir and Vanir, but most especially to Óðinn, Bragi, Kvasir, Víðarr, Freyja, and Thor for their inspiration.

# Table of Contents

Preface .................................................................xiii

Introduction to the Meters ...............................................xv

The Types of Poems in this Book .........................................xxi

## Chapter 1: Hallowing and Warding ........................................1
    Shortest Hammer Hallowing ..........................................1
    Short Hammer Hallowing .............................................1
    Long Hammer Hallowing ..............................................2
    Fire and Ice Warding ...............................................3
    Four Dwarves Warding ...............................................4
    Unattested Dwarves Addition ........................................4
    Short Water Warding ................................................5
    Extended Water Warding .............................................5
    Spear Warding ......................................................6
    Other Spear Warding ................................................6
    Fire Warding .......................................................7
    Sword Warding ......................................................7
    Other Sword Warding ................................................7
    Mead Warding .......................................................8
    Nine Worlds and Elements Hallowing .................................8
    Concluding Statement ...............................................9

## Chapter 2: Poetic Tales ................................................10
    The Binding of Fenrir .............................................10
    The Brísingamen ...................................................13
    Building Asgard's Wall ............................................19
    The Duel ..........................................................22
    Freyr and Gerð ....................................................27
    Gunnlaðarljóð .....................................................28
    Iðunn's Abduction .................................................31
    The Mead Quest ....................................................35
    The Six Treasures .................................................37
    Thor's Visit to Geirröð ...........................................39
    Valhalla ..........................................................42

## Chapter 3: Short Calls .................................................46
    Aegir Call ........................................................46
    Aegir's Daughters Call ............................................46
    Aesir Call ........................................................47

Álfar Call ......................................................................................47
Ancestors Call ...............................................................................48
Ask and Embla Call .....................................................................48
Auðumbla Call .............................................................................49
Baldur Call....................................................................................49
Bestla Call .....................................................................................50
Borr Call .......................................................................................50
Bragi Call ......................................................................................51
Brokk and Eitri Call ....................................................................51
Búri Call .......................................................................................52
Dag Call ........................................................................................52
Dísir Call ......................................................................................53
Dvergar Call .................................................................................53
Einherjar Call...............................................................................54
Eir Call .........................................................................................54
Forseti Call....................................................................................55
Freyja Call.....................................................................................55
Freyr Call ......................................................................................56
Frigg Call ......................................................................................56
Frigg's Handmaidens Call ...........................................................57
Gefjon Call ...................................................................................57
Gerð Call ......................................................................................58
Gríð Call.......................................................................................58
Gunnlöð Call ...............................................................................59
Heimdall Call ..............................................................................59
Heimdall's Mothers Call..............................................................60
Hel Call ........................................................................................60
Helgi Call .....................................................................................61
Hermóð Call ................................................................................61
Höð Call .......................................................................................62
Hœnir Call ...................................................................................62
Honored Dead Call......................................................................63
Iðunn Call ....................................................................................63
Ívaldi's Sons Call ..........................................................................64
Jörð Call .......................................................................................64
Kvasir Call ....................................................................................65
Landvættir Call ............................................................................65
Lóðurr Call ...................................................................................66
Loki Call .......................................................................................66
Máni Call......................................................................................67
Mímir Call (God) ........................................................................67
Mímir Call (Etin) ........................................................................68
Móði and Magni Call..................................................................68
Nanna Call ...................................................................................69
Nerthus Call .................................................................................69

 Njörð Call ........................................................................70
 Nornir Call .......................................................................70
 Nótt Call ..........................................................................71
 Óðinn Call ........................................................................71
 Others Call .......................................................................72
 Rán Call ...........................................................................72
 Rind Call ..........................................................................73
 Sága Call ..........................................................................73
 Sif Call .............................................................................74
 Sigyn Call .........................................................................74
 Sigmund Call ....................................................................75
 Sigurð Call ........................................................................75
 Skaði Call .........................................................................76
 Sunna Call ........................................................................76
 Thor Call ..........................................................................77
 Thrúð Call ........................................................................77
 Týr Call ............................................................................78
 Ull Call .............................................................................78
 Váli Call ...........................................................................79
 Valkyrjur Call ...................................................................79
 Vanir Call .........................................................................80
 Vár Call ............................................................................80
 Víðarr Call ........................................................................81
 Vili and Vé Call .................................................................81
 Völund Call ......................................................................82
 Zisa Call ...........................................................................82

## Chapter 4: Long Calls ................................................................83
 Call to Óðinn ....................................................................83
 Call to Freyja ....................................................................84
 Call to Thor ......................................................................86

## Chapter 5: Ritual Dramas .........................................................88
 The Abduction of Iðunn ..................................................88
 The Creation of the Six Treasures ....................................98
 The Winning of the Mead ..............................................110

## Chapter 6: Praise Poems ..........................................................118
 A Tale of Wisdom's Well ................................................118
 The Drápa of Battle Cry .................................................120
 A Drápa for Formal Sumbel ..........................................123
 Fólksdrápa ......................................................................126
 Mead for Camp Netimus ...............................................130
 An Offering to Nettie .....................................................132

 Pagan Praise to Freyr .................................................................. 134
 Sumartímadrápa........................................................................ 136
 Thor Processional Chant .......................................................... 139
 An Ull Poem .............................................................................. 141
 Vetrartímadrápa ........................................................................ 142
 Yggdrasilsdrápa ......................................................................... 144

## Chapter 7: Stand-alone Sumbel Toasts ....................... 150
 Aegir Toasts................................................................................ 150
 Aesir Toast.................................................................................. 150
 Ancestor Toast (General) ......................................................... 151
 Ancestor Toast (Personal) ........................................................ 151
 Baldur Toast .............................................................................. 152
 Forseti Toast .............................................................................. 152
 Frau Holle Toast........................................................................ 152
 Freyja Toasts .............................................................................. 153
 Freyr Toasts ............................................................................... 153
 Frigg Toast ................................................................................. 154
 Heimdall Toast .......................................................................... 154
 Iðunn Toast................................................................................ 155
 Óðinn Toast ............................................................................... 155
 Sunna Toast............................................................................... 156
 Thor Toast.................................................................................. 156
 Týr Toast .................................................................................... 157
 Ull Toast .................................................................................... 157
 Wayfarer Toast .......................................................................... 157
 Wights Toasts............................................................................. 158

## Chapter 8: Sumbel Toast Sequences ........................... 159
 A Disting Sequence................................................................... 159
 A Summerfinding Sequence .................................................... 160
 A May Day Sequence................................................................ 161
 A Midsummer Sequence .......................................................... 161
 A Freyfaxi Sequence ................................................................. 163
 A Winterfinding Sequence ...................................................... 164
 A Harvest Sequence .................................................................. 165
 A Winternights Sequence ........................................................ 166
 Another Winternights Sequence............................................. 167
 A Fallen Heroes Sequence ....................................................... 168
 A Mothernight Sequence......................................................... 169
 A Yule Sequence........................................................................ 170
 Another Disting Sequence....................................................... 171
 Another Midsummer Sequence............................................... 172

## Chapter 9: Prayers .................................................... 174
Aegir Prayer .................................................... 174
Ancestors Prayer ............................................. 174
Baldur Prayer .................................................. 174
Bragi Prayer .................................................... 175
Dag Prayer ...................................................... 175
Eir Prayer ........................................................ 176
Forseti Prayer .................................................. 176
Freyja Prayer ................................................... 176
Freyr Prayer .................................................... 177
Frigg Prayer .................................................... 177
Heimdall Prayer .............................................. 177
Hel Prayer ....................................................... 178
Hœnir Prayer .................................................. 178
Iðunn Prayer ................................................... 179
Jörð Prayer ...................................................... 179
Kvasir Prayer ................................................... 179
Landvættir Prayer ............................................ 180
Máni Prayer .................................................... 180
Mímir Prayer ................................................... 180
Njörð Prayer ................................................... 181
Nótt Prayer ..................................................... 181
Óðinn Prayer .................................................. 182
Sif Prayer ........................................................ 182
Sunna Prayer ................................................... 182
Thor Prayer .................................................... 183
Týr Prayer ....................................................... 183
Ull Prayer ....................................................... 183
Váli Prayer ...................................................... 184
Vár Prayer ....................................................... 184
Víðarr Prayer ................................................... 185
Eirik's Hymn .................................................. 185

## Chapter 10: Short Charms ............................... 186
Waking Stave ................................................... 186
Sun Stave ........................................................ 186
Washing Stave ................................................. 186
Food Stave ...................................................... 187
Drink Stave ..................................................... 187
Moon Stave ..................................................... 187
Sleeping Stave ................................................. 187
For Collecting a Blót Tine ............................... 188
For Returning a Blót Tine ............................... 188
For Pouring Out a Blót Bowl .......................... 188

An Opening Call for Sumbel ..................................................189
A Closing Call for Sumbel ....................................................189

## Chapter 11: Other Poems .............................................190
Öfundarmál .........................................................................190
Beer in Midgard...................................................................192
Fyrir Íslensku Landvættirnar ...............................................193
Heathen Pride .....................................................................195
New Year's Renewal..............................................................196
Nine Noble Virtues...............................................................197
Perseverance ........................................................................200
A Valentine's Day Poem .......................................................202
Wrath of Frost Giants? ........................................................203
Wrath of a Tiny Etin?...........................................................204
A Yule Poem ........................................................................204
Rise and Reach the Gods!.....................................................205

## Index .................................................................................211

# Preface

This book is an effort to restore the ancient meters and forms so that they can live again and fulfill their traditional purposes again. It is also a challenge, one that declares that the dead end of modern free verse doesn't have to be the end of poetry, that the way forward is by a return to tradition.

The poems in this book fulfill that mission by leading through example. True to its name, the majority of poems in this collection were written for use in many different parts of heathen ritual. Among other things, the poems here hallow space, call to the gods, memorialize heroes and ancestors, give praise, and bring the power of ritual to everyday life. They educate, inspire, and help one align with higher principles.

Many of these Viking poems have previously appeared on my blog ("The Skaldic Eagle" at press time, formerly called "Eirik Westcoat, Skald"), but I won't attempt to recount their original appearances there. Other poems have been published elsewhere, and these I will recount. "Öfundarmál" first appeared in *Idunna* 96 (Summer 2013). "A Tale of Wisdom's Well" first appeared in *Idunna* 97 (Autumn 2013). Three of the poems have won victory in skaldic competitions at the annual East Coast Thing: "The Six Treasures" in 2011, "Yggdrasilsdrápa" in 2012, and "A Tale of Wisdom's Well" in 2013.

This book is laid out with the following structure. First, there is an introduction to the meters that I use, followed by a section on the types of poems, so that the poems can then be read uninterrupted in the main text as follows:
- Chapter 1 presents short pieces that can be used for hallowing and warding ritual space through various means.
- Chapter 2 features poetic retellings of prose tales, most of which appeared in Snorri's *Prose Edda* but did not have counterparts in the *Poetic Edda*. My award-winning poem, "The Six Treasures," is in this chapter.

- Chapter 3 features a nearly exhaustive set of two-stanza calls to many gods and heroes, ideal for ritual use.
- Chapter 4 contains longer calls to Óðinn, Freyja, and Thor.
- Chapter 5 contains three ritual dramas — dialogue only, you'll need to supply stage directions for performance.
- Chapter 6 demonstrates another function of the ancient skald — formal praise poems to those who deserve them. My two other award-winning poems, "Yggdrasilsdrápa" and "A Tale of Wisdom's Well," are in this chapter. "Thor Processional Chant" debuted at East Coast Thing 2016, with music developed by Josh Rood. (These first six chapters are roughly in the order that they might be used in a heathen blessing.)
- Chapter 7 is similar, except these are short pieces written as sumbel toasts to gods, ancestors, heroes, and other wights.
- Chapter 8 also contains sumbel toasts, except these were written and recited as sequences presented over the three rounds of a heathen sumbel.
- Chapter 9 is something unusual for heathenry: prayers to the gods.
- Chapter 10 presents various short charms for waking, eating, sleeping, and similar for use in daily life.
- Chapter 11 finishes the book with various heathen-related poetry that didn't fit elsewhere.

Many of the poems, especially those in chapters 2 and 6, are lengthy enough to stand on their own and be recited in a hall or around a campfire to entertain or inspire an audience. They were written to be heard! Of course, I can't put a live campfire performance in a book. However, I'm doing the next best thing: offering quality digital audio recordings of many of the poems — look for them available separately.

In addition to poetry that you can recite in your own rituals, you will find beauty, inspiration, lore, and more in these pages. Through poetry, Óðrœrir returns to Midgard for both Ash and Elm.

# Introduction to the Meters

A brief explanation of the meters I have used is in order, although this is not the place for going into exhaustive detail on how to write modern English versions of the ancient meters. Also, keep in mind that these are modern English versions. They are not and do not purport to be "clones" of the Old Norse or Old English versions, as such a thing is neither possible nor desirable due to the differences in the languages. Additionally, many of my poems may show some intricacies that aren't described here.

*Fornyrðislag.* This is the simplest of the meters and is easily recognized in this book by the eight-line stanzas of the poems that use it. I use it quite frequently. It is based on the elder form of the same name, a name which roughly means "meter of ancient words." This is the form used by many of the poems of the *Poetic Edda* (such as *Völuspá* and *Thrymskviða*), and is also the form that Tolkien used in *The Legend of Sigurd and Gudrun*. Each line contains two fully stressed syllables and generally a minimum of four syllables overall. (Some of my older poems will have three-syllable lines.) The first stress of the second line of each pair must alliterate with either, or both, of the stresses in the first line of the pair. The second stress of the second line must not alliterate with the first stress of the second line but may optionally alliterate with one of the stresses in the first line. Unstressed syllables are not counted for alliteration purposes, and the number of them in each line is usually two to four but can be more or less than that. All vowels are considered to alliterate with each other. Inspired by Old Norse and Old English practice, I treat the consonant clusters *sk*, *sp*, *st*, and *sh* as only alliterating with themselves, not with each other or with *s* by itself. Here is an example of two lines of *fornyrðislag* from my poem "Heathen Pride":

> We are hearty heathens,
> happy and proud.

You can see that the h-sounds of *hearty, heathens,* and *happy* all alliterate in accord with the rules just described, as it is the first syllable of each of these words that carries the stress. The p-sound of *proud,* which is the last stressed syllable of these lines, does not alliterate. (Pronouns such as *we,* and forms of the verb *to be* don't usually bear stress in this sort of poetry, but there are exceptions.) Add another three pairs of lines such as these to get a full stanza.

*Runhent.* This is a *fornyrðislag* variant in which the final syllables of a pair of lines are stressed and fully rhyme. Its name means something like "run-rhymed." Historically, its most significant occurrence was in Egill Skallagrímsson's poem "Head Ransom." Here is an example of two lines of *runhent* from my poem "Yggdrasilsdrápa":

> With worlds all nine,
> that Wood does shine.

That poem is the only one of this collection to use *runhent* systematically, and it does so in the refrain stanzas.

*Anglo-Saxon.* This is quite similar to *fornyrðislag*, but with mainly stylistic changes. The half-lines are strictly four syllables minimum, never less. The main difference from *fornyrðislag* is that it is not broken into stanzas — it runs continuously one line after the other. Also, whereas the two lines in a *fornyrðislag* pair are printed separately, they are here printed together to make a single line (sometimes called a long line) in this format. As an example, if the above lines from "Heathen Pride" were printed in this form, they would look like this:

> We are hearty heathens, happy and proud.

This is how Tolkien's verse in *The Fall of Arthur* is rendered, except that the caesura between half-lines is shown by extra space between them. I, however, think the poems look better without it, and the clever reader would be able to figure out where those breaks occurred based on the stress and alliteration. In this book, the form is used only for the prayers in chapter 10 and one of the poems in chapter 12. Historically, the Anglo-Saxons did not develop a plethora of verse forms the way that Old Norse poetry did, and generally used this form for their poetry, running one long line after another without stanza breaks for as long as needed in a particular poem. *Beowulf* and the *Old English Rune Poem* are excellent examples of the form in addition to being poems that modern heathens should know. The historical *Anglo-Saxon* meter tended to have more syllables per line than the historical *fornyrðislag*, but this was mainly due to the differences in the languages. As my modern *fornyrðislag* and *Anglo-Saxon* are both written in modern English, they don't have this difference in average syllable count.

*Ljóðaháttr.* This is another fairly simple meter (though slightly more complex than *fornyrðislag*), and it is easily recognized in this book by the six-line stanzas of the poems that use it. Its name means "song-meter." It is quite common in this book. This meter is also used by many of the poems in the *Poetic Edda* (such as *Hávamál* and *Vafþrúðnismál*). The basic unit is a half-stanza of three lines. The first two lines are as in *fornyrðislag*, although the first line can be as short as two or three syllables total. The third line of each half-stanza is called a full line, and usually has three stresses, any two of which will alliterate. The structure of the half-stanza is repeated to make a full stanza of six lines. Here is an example of three lines (a half-stanza) of *ljóðaháttr* from a hail to Óðinn:

> Hail to Óðinn,
> highest of Aesir,
> for giving self to self.

You can see that the first two lines are like in *fornyrðislag*. The h-sound of *hail* alliterates with the h-sound of *highest*. Also, there is secondary alliteration, where the vowel-sound of

Óðinn alliterates with the vowel-sound of *Aesir*. (I tend to use such secondary alliteration far more frequently than the ancient poets did, in both *fornyrðislag* and *ljóðahátt*.) In the third line, the stresses are on the g-sound of *giving* and the s-sound of both instances of *self*, and thus the alliteration is on the two s-sounds. Add another three lines such as these, and you get a full stanza.

*Galdralag*. This is an important variant of *ljóðahátt* that I occasionally use, especially in sumbel toasts. Its name means "meter of magic." This occurs whenever one or more additional full lines follow the usual single full line in a half-stanza of *ljóðahátt*. (Examples of *galdralag* occur most frequently in *Hávamál* but are found in other poems of the *Poetic Edda* as well.) Often (but not always), this additional full line will repeat the preceding full line but with a slight variation of some sort. Here's an example of an extra line added to the Óðinn hail to make *galdralag*:

> Hail to Óðinn,
> highest of Aesir,
> for giving self to self,
> for giving Mead to Man.

You can see that the fourth line is a clone of the third, with only two words changed. The rules for alliteration in a full line still apply. It's not always necessary for the lines to look so similar. I could have done this instead:

> Hail to Óðinn,
> highest of Aesir;
> by giving self to self,
> he won and wrote the Runes.

It's still *galdralag* that way, even though it lacks the repetitive character. [For more on the historical uses of this meter, I refer the reader to my scholarly article, "The Goals of *Galdralag*: Identifying the Historical Instances and uses of the

Metre" in the Viking Society's *Saga-Book* 40 (2016), pages 69–90.]

*Dróttkvætt.* If you have ever heard that one of the meters of Viking poetry was fiendishly difficult, this is the meter you heard about. Its name means "court-meter." Like *fornyrðislag*, it is written in pairs of lines, eight lines total to a stanza. Unlike *fornyrðislag*, each line has exactly six syllables and usually three main stresses. Two stressed syllables in the first line will alliterate with the first stressed syllable of the second line. (Secondary alliteration is possible but seldom used since meeting the rhyme requirements must come before it.) The first line features a slant rhyme between the last syllable and one of the preceding syllables. (A slant rhyme is one where the consonant sounds match but the vowel sounds differ, such as in *code* and *made*.) The second line features a full rhyme between the last syllable and one of the preceding syllables. (This is the kind of rhyme that everyone is familiar with, such as in *might* and *sight*.) Here is an example from my poem "A Tale of Wisdom's Well":

> With mead I rightly made
> from might of lore tonight.

The alliteration is on the m-sound, the slant rhyme is *mead/made*, and the full rhyme is *might/tonight*. Just like in *fornyrðislag*, add another three pairs of lines such as these to get a full stanza. "A Tale of Wisdom's Well" is the only poem in this book to use *dróttkvætt*. (My modern *dróttkvætt* differs a bit from the older style in the placement of alliteration and rhymes in order to accommodate language differences.)

Now for some final notes on the meters. In all the examples here, the stress was on the first syllable of multi-syllable words such as *hearty, heathens, happy, giving, highest*, etc. This isn't always the case. Most prefixes in modern English aren't stressed. Thus, in words like *become, provide*, and *away*, the stress is on the second syllable, not the first. (Thus, it is on *c*, *v*, and *w* instead of *b*, *p*, and *a*, respectively.)

Not sure where the stress is supposed to fall on a word? Consult a dictionary — I do so frequently. Also, to make sure there is no confusion, it is the sound that matters, not the spelling, for the purposes of alliteration. Although spelled differently, *kick* and *come* alliterate because they start with the same sound; *cent* and *come* do not alliterate — their initial sounds are different although they start with the same letter. Regarding stanza length, the old poetry wasn't always as consistent as described above. Longer and shorter stanzas occurred. I am consistent with stanza lengths, with the exception of my short calls, ritual dramas, and sumbel toasts — in these cases, it is usually more appropriate to break the poetry between calls, speakers, and toasts instead.

Some words may be said about the history of these meters. Ultimately, they would all go back to a form of long line verse common to the Germanic peoples (roughly around the beginning of the Common Era but perhaps earlier as well) that was probably not broken into stanzas — something more or less like the *Anglo-Saxon* form described above, except that the language would have been at the stage of Proto-Germanic or Common Germanic, languages that had more syllables per word on average than the descendant Old English and Old Norse languages — and so its long line, however exactly it worked, would have had a higher syllable count. In what became Old Norse culture, that Proto-Germanic long line developed into *fornyrðislag*. From there, by various changes, including the addition of rhymes, the other forms — *ljóðahátt, galdralag, runhent, dróttkvætt,* and more — arose, but exactly how and why this happened is still a matter debated by scholars.

# The Types of Poems in this Book

Some brief remarks on the different types of poems I write are also in order. They vary in form and purpose, and here I give descriptions of the various types. Any of the types can use any of the meters described above.

*Drápur.* A *drápa* is poem with one or more refrains. Usually, it is also a praise poem. In the Old Norse period, it would generally be chieftains, jarls, or kings who would be the recipient of the praise. These could be as long as the intended recipient could bear. A poem by Þjóðólfr Arnórsson was called "Sexstefja," meaning literally "Six Refrains." The fragment of it that survives is only thirty some stanzas, and probably ran much longer than that in its entirety. *Drápur* were often written in the difficult and prestigious *dróttkvætt* meter but could be written in any of the traditional Old Norse meters. The most famous *drápa* today from the Viking Age is "Head Ransom" by Egill Skallagrímsson. It is twenty stanzas with two different refrains. It was written in *runhent* as mentioned above. Most of my *drápur* in this book have the word *drápa* in their titles. Following a tradition I encountered in some translations and editions of Old Norse poetry, the refrains are italicized in my poems.

*Flokkar.* A *flokk* (meaning "group, company, host" and cognate with English *flock*) is distinguished from a *drápa* simply by a lack of refrains. Like a *drápa*, it can be written in any of the traditional Old Norse meters. According to Lee Hollander, Egill Skallagrímssson's "Lay of Arinbjörn," in praise of Egill's dear friend, was a *flokk*, probably in the 40 to 60 stanza range. In my modern usage, I will probably restrict the label of *flokk* to praise poems only, as the vast majority of my poems don't have refrains, and specifically labelling them as *flokkar* seems redundant.

*Hallowings.* Although many Asatruar no longer practice the hallowing of the ritual space, some still do, and I have written a couple hammer hallowings of various lengths in both *ljóðahátt* and *fornyrðislag*, as well as other hallowings that make use of different ritual tools such as swords, spears, fire, etc.

*Lore narratives.* In this group are those poems I write which retell a story from the Old Norse mythology. Generally, my writing efforts are directed to those stories that do not have poetic versions in the *Poetic Edda*. My poems "The Six Treasures," "Mead Quest," "The Binding of Fenrir," and so forth fall into this group. If one is doing a *blót* ("blessing") to a particular god or goddess, reading a story about him or her would be appropriate during the rite. For instance, one might read the "Six Treasures" during a *blót* to either Thor or the Dwarves. The lore narratives that I have written are generally in either *fornyrðislag* or *ljóðahátt*.

*Calls to gods and others.* In a *blót*, it is customary to include a call to the particular being or beings one is honoring. I have written a vast number of two-stanza calls in *ljóðahátt* that make use of the existing lore. For the major gods and goddess about whom we have a significant amount of lore, calls of much greater length can be written, and I have written a few of these. Although *fornyrðislag* would be a perfectly fine meter for a call, all the calls I've written are in *ljóðahátt*. It just turned out that way.

*Praise poems.* Simply put, a poem in praise of a god, goddess, wight, or something else entirely. These are distinguished according to whether they are *drápur* or *flokkar*. Such praise poems could be used as sumbel toasts, but are often suitable for being read as part of the centerpiece of a rite. For instance, "Vetrartímadrápa," which is a poem in praise of Wintertime, was first recited as part of a Winter Nights blessing by the Hearth of Yggdrasil.

*Ritual dramas.* To give just two examples, *Skírnismál* and *Lokasenna* from the *Poetic Edda* are poems with multiple characters and dialogue. On reading them, one could very easily get the impression that they were meant to be recited in front of an audience by multiple people who were perhaps doing some acting along with it. Inspired by that possibility (which is explored in scholarly detail by Terry Gunnell in *The Origins of Drama in Scandinavia*), the short ritual dramas that I write have a narrator who speaks in *fornyrðislag* and various characters who speak in *ljóðahátt*. These are also quite suited for use in ritual (hence the name) with different people reciting each role. The one that I wrote based on Snorri's tale of the abduction of Iðunn was performed by the Hearth of Yggdrasil at one of their Midsummer blessings.

*Sumbel toasts*. The most usual format for a sumbel is to have three rounds: the first is dedicated to the gods, the second to heroes and ancestors, and the third to participant's choice — boasts, toasts, or even oaths on occasion. In each round, each participant will usually speak some words of praise, honor, or remembrance, followed by a drink from the sumbel horn. Sumbel toasts can be as short as "Hail Thor!" or longer and more involved. Most are usually spoken in an impromptu fashion. However, poetry or song is also quite appropriate. Generally, the sumbel toasts I've written are one or two stanzas in *ljóðahátt* or *galdralag*, although I have written a few in *fornyrðislag*. The longest poems I've written specifically as sumbel toasts are a trio of seven-stanza *drápur* in *ljóðahátt*. (They are combined into a single *drápa* in this book.) Many of my sumbel toasts were deliberately written as sequences that I recited in the three successive rounds of a single sumbel, so those sequences usually contain three toasts, one for each round. Some of the sequences contain multiple toasts per round.

*Prayers*. This is perhaps a provocative category to include, as many would feel that prayer gets a bad name from the various monotheistic religions. Yet the polytheists of old had prayers, whether Greek, Roman, Celtic, Vedic, and so forth. Unfortunately, heathen Germanic liturgy didn't survive the conversion. So, I have written some modern prayers to the gods. All of the prayers in this book are written in the *Anglo-Saxon* meter with nine lines each. This includes "Eirik's Hymn," which is my loose, heathenized translation/interpretation of a piece of Old English poetry known as *Cædmon's Hymn*. Though it is quite different from the other prayers, I have included it with them nonetheless.

*Charms*. The charms in this book are short pieces of poetry intended for frequent ritual use with daily activities such as waking, sleeping, eating, etc. One of them, "For Pouring Out a Blót Bowl," is a poetic expansion of a modern heathen custom — the pouring out of an offering with what are now traditional words: "From the gods to the earth to us, from us to the earth to the gods — a gift for a gift — hail!" Once I realized that the first part of it was a valid *galdralag* couplet of full lines, I simply had to write a stanza for it.

Here are some final notes for those who would recite and use the poems. Generally, one may change things from plural to singular in the calls and prayers without damaging the meter (such as replacing *us* with *me*, and *we* with *I*). I have generally left the Old Norse names as they are, with the accent marks and strange characters (as I find most anglicizings to be rather ugly), although with some changes to make things easier for those not familiar with the language. In word-initial position, I use *th* instead of *þ* (that is, *Thrúð* instead of *Þrúð*), *ae* instead of *æ*, and *oe* instead of *œ*. I have dropped the nominative *-r* ending in places where it is difficult to pronounce (such as *Heimdall* instead of *Heimdallr*) but have retained it where it will not cause problems (such as in *Freyr*). That particular change makes the names easier to use with English grammar. A few names (such as *Thor*, *Midgard*, and *Asgard*) are rendered in the familiar anglicized forms (instead of *Þórr*, *Miðgarðr*, and *Ásgarðr*). One may use a pronunciation guide for Old Norse or Modern Icelandic according to preference.

# Chapter 1: Hallowing and Warding

*Shortest Hammer Hallowing*

> Hammer within,
> Hammer without,
> hallow our holy stead;
> bane of etins,
> banish evil:
> watch and ward our stead.

*Short Hammer Hallowing*

> Hammer in the North,
> hallow our stead
> and ward against
> wights of evil.
> Hammer in the East,
> hallow our stead
> and ward against
> wights of evil.
>
> Hammer in the South,
> hallow our stead
> and ward against
> wights of evil.
> Hammer in the West,
> hallow our stead
> and ward against
> wights of evil.

Hammer above us,
hallow our stead
and ward against
wights of evil.
Hammer below us,
hallow our stead
and ward against
wights of evil.

## *Long Hammer Hallowing*

Hammer of Thor,
Hammer in the North,
hallow our holy stead;
bane of etins,
banish evil:
watch and ward our stead.

Hammer of Thor,
Hammer in the East,
hallow our holy stead;
bane of etins,
banish evil:
watch and ward our stead.

Hammer of Thor,
Hammer in the South,
hallow our holy stead;
bane of etins,
banish evil:
watch and ward our stead.

Hammer of Thor,
Hammer in the West,

hallow our holy stead;
bane of etins,
banish evil:
watch and ward our stead.

Hammer of Thor,
Hammer above us,
hallow our holy stead;
bane of etins,
banish evil:
watch and ward our stead.

Hammer of Thor,
Hammer below us,
hallow our holy stead;
bane of etins,
banish evil:
watch and ward our stead.

## *Fire and Ice Warding*

I call on the Fire
that fiercely burns,
a blazing brand
that's born of Muspell;
with primal power
I prepare this stead
and hold it holy
for helpful wights.

I call on the Ice
that's always cold,
a freezing flow
that's formed in Nifl;

with primal power
I prepare this stead
and hold it holy
for helpful wights.

## *Four Dwarves Warding*

Hail to Norðri,
your name we call;
hallow here now
our holy stead.
Hail to Austri,
answer our call;
hallow here now
our holy stead.

Hail to Suðri,
sincerely we call;
hallow here now
our holy stead.
Hail to Vestri,
with vigor we call;
hallow here now
our holy stead.

## *Unattested Dwarves Addition*

Hail to Uppi,
eagerly we call;
hallow here now
our holy stead.
Hail to Niðri,
with need we call;

hallow here now
our holy stead.

## Short Water Warding

I sprinkle water
— a splash from the well —
to hallow and hold
our holy stead;
the power of Wyrd
will ward us now
and keep secure
our kindred work.

## Extended Water Warding

From the Well of Hvergelmir,
this water I sprinkle
to hallow and hold
our holy stead.
That primal power
makes pure this realm;
for working our will,
well it cleanses.

From the Well of Mímir,
this water I sprinkle
to hallow and hold
our holy stead.
The might and main
of memory and wisdom
is boon and blessing
to the best of wights.

From the Well of Urð,
this water I sprinkle
to hallow and hold
our holy stead.
The workings of Wyrd
will ward us now
and keep secure
our kindred work.

## *Spear Warding*

This gar guards now
our garth tonight;
it hallows and holds
our holy stead.
The weapon wards
by will this realm
and keeps secure
our kindred work.

## *Other Spear Warding*

With spear, I circle
and bespell this stead
for boons and blessings
from the best of wights.
By steel is made
a state that's holy
and warded well
for our work today.

## Fire Warding

This brightly burning
and blazing fire
hallows and holds
our holy stead.
These boundaries meet
by brand are marked
and kept secure
for our kindred work.

## Sword Warding

A battle-icicle
I brandish now
to hallow and hold
this holy stead.
By steel is made
a state of welcome
for boons and blessings
from the best of wights.

## Other Sword Warding

With sword, I circle
this site of work
and mark with main
its mighty boundaries.
By strength of steel,
this stead is blessed
and hallowed with will
for helpful wights.

*Mead Warding*

Through words and will
my wode is stirred;
with skaldic skill
I scour this realm.
The might and main
of the mead Óðrœrir
hallows and holds
this holy stead.

*Nine Worlds and Elements Hallowing*

I hallow here now
this holy stead
by rightly naming
the realms and elements,
for our work is warded
by their wealful order.
To the North is Niflheim
and its needful Ice.

To the South is Muspellsheim
and its searing Fire.
To the West is Vanaheim
and its vigorous Yeast.
To the East is Jötunheim
and its acid Venom.
Above is Ljósálfheim
and its lofty Air.

Below is Svartálfheim
and its solid Iron.

Highest is Asgard
and its holy Salt.
Lowest is Hel
and its liquid Water.
In the middle is Midgard
and its mighty Earth.

The realms and elements
are rightfully ordered,
as Óðinn deemed
in elder days.
I've recalled creation,
thus keeping its power
rightfully present
in our ritual today.

## *Concluding Statement*

Now is hallowed
our holy stead
for the work of weal
that well we start.
By might and main,
we're meetly warded
against the ways
and wights unholy.

# Chapter 2: Poetic Tales

## *The Binding of Fenrir*

The ale of Ygg
I eagerly brewed,
and here I pour that poem.
Of Fenrir's binding
and famous Týr,
that spell I speak to all.

Loki and Angrboða,
they lay together
and a gruesome three they begat.
A woman half-corpse,
a wolf, and a serpent:
these offspring were destined for doom.

The wolf alone
waxed in Asgard,
fed by trusty Týr.
But fast he grew
and was greatly feared;
the Aesir sought an answer.

Fenrir they chose
to fetter and bind,
to save their home from harm.
They bid him try
and test his strength
against the chains they chose.

With a mighty thrash,
he threw off Leyðing:
that fetter failed to hold!
With a mighty strain,
he struck off Drómi:
that fetter failed to hold!

Freyr's friend,
fair Skírnir,
from dwarves he fetched a fetter.
Subtle runes,
six in all,
were blended to form that bond:

woman's beard,
bear's sinews,
mountain's mighty roots,
fish's breath,
bird's spittle,
and cat's noise of falling feet.

Soft and smooth
like a silken ribbon,
yet firm and fast as well:
the Aesir wished
the wolf to try
Gleipnir against his strength.

The wolf had guessed
that guile and tricks
were used to form that fetter;
a pledge as proof
to place in his mouth,
he demanded from the mighty Aesir.

And almost all
the Aesir refused
to pledge the price required,
but honorable Týr
offered his hand,
the weregild the wolf desired.

With the slender band,
they bound the wolf:
that fetter firmly held!
But the wolf's price
was paid by Týr:
in lying he lost his hand.

On Lyngvi Isle
in Lake Amsvartnir,
Fenrir is firmly held
with Gleipnir by Gelgja
on Gjöll attached,
thrust by Thviti in ground.

A mighty sword
in his mouth is thrust;
that burden stops his bite.
Howling horribly,
Hope from his mouth
runs as a river of spit.

Fast today
that fetter holds,
and ever after still,
until that day
of terrible dark:
the time of Ragnarök.

## The Brísingamen

Might with metals
is the main of dwarves,
and as good as any
are Grérr, Álfrigg,
Dvalinn, and Berling
in doing that work.
In a rock they lived
and wrought their craft.

Word of their work
had wended far,
flying to Asgard
and Freyja's ears.
In a day of wandering,
the Dís of the Vanir
came in the cave
of these crafty dwarves.

The eyes of Freyja
then angled upon
a gleaming necklace
of gold and amber.
'Twas Brísingamen,
the best of jewels,
and Fólkvang's lady
was flaming with lust.

The greatest treasure
of gold and silver
she offered to them
to own that jewel.
But the dwarves declined

and deemed her money
a rather poor price
for parting with it.

The craftsmen then
declared their price:
her body would be
the best exchange.
In love and lust
she'd lay with them
for one night each
to win that jewel.

For nights all four,
her nubile form
sated the lust
of salacious dwarves;
furtively then
Freyja returned,
back to her bower
with the beautiful jewel.

But Loki had witnessed
that long exchange
of carnal delights,
craving mischief.
As with Sif before,
he would seek a way
to slip inside
and seize her treasure.

Alone at night,
Loki then searched.
In form of fly

he flitted around,
hoping to find
a hole to enter.
Up by the gable
he gained his entrance.

Freyja was found
by Farbauti's son,
soundly sleeping
inside her bower.
Above her breast
was Brísingamen;
beneath her neck
was the needed clasp.

Into form of flea
the feisty one
then changed and bit
her cheek with malice.
Startled she stirred,
then stretched and turned.
The clasp exposed,
he carried it off.

When morning came,
Mardöll awoke
and noticed now
her necklace gone.
Unbroken but open
was her bower door.
Was it Byleist's brother
who'd been inside?

To the hall of Hár
she hastened for news,
asking if any
had answers to give.
Where was Loki
or the winsome jewel?
The gathered Aesir
together mooted.

The sly one was seen
sneaking away,
carrying something
he was keeping hidden.
Whither went he
wending quickly?
Silent Víðarr
to Singasteinn pointed.

On hearing that news,
Heimdall the white
stood and started
and stammered almost.
As warden of Bifröst
he watches the realms,
yet mischief's maker
he'd missed completely.

The son of sisters
then sought to redeem
his failure of sight
by finding the thief.
Great Gullintanni
would regain that jewel,

his service pledged
to Sýr for honor.

Valiant Vindlér
ventured to Singasteinn,
a skerry far out
and scoured by winds.
To reach that rock,
from radiant Ull
he received a bone
to surf the waves.

A seal was swimming
in the sea nearby,
splashing around
in sparkling water.
A shape-shifter
he'd surely found,
Sýr's servant knew,
on seeing its eyes.

The burly brute
then barked in anger
when he realized
the watchman saw him.
Under the waves
he went and vanished,
leaving Heimdall
alone on the rock.

But Heimdall was skilled
in the hidden magics
and knew the charms
to change his shape.

He rowned some runes
in a rhythmic chant;
to shape of seal
he shifted his form.

In the drink he dove,
down after the fiend,
flapping flippers
in furious pursuit.
The warrior warden
in water moved quick
and nearly caught
crafty Nálarson.

Loki evaded
and leapt on the rock
to face and fight
his furious pursuer.
The bouncing blubbers
in battle then crashed,
a serious struggle
on Singasteinn.

Heimdall with his head
then hammered Loki.
It served him well
as a sword of might,
for the top of his tree,
containing authority,
availed against Loki
for victory on the rock.

Byleist's brother
was beat at last;

regained for Gefn
was the gleaming jewel.
Loki was bound
and led back home.
Heimdall's honor
was healed through glory.

Now that necklace
is on noble Freyja;
it brightens her beauty,
that best of jewels,
for Mardöll is honored
by mighty treasures,
that glorious mother
of Gersemi and Hnoss.

## *Building Asgard's Wall*

Silence I seek
for saying my tale
of the master mason
who meant to build
for the garth of the Gods
the greatest of walls;
with Ygg's ale now
I utter my words.

Midgard was made
and mighty Valhöll;
for proof against
the passage of etins,
the Aesir sought
a solid defense;

a builder offered
the best of walls.

The sun and moon
he sought as payment
and Freyja to wed
as fairest wife;
the Aesir allowed
only a winter —
if unfinished the fort,
then forfeit his wage.

Alone must he labor,
allowed no help;
an exception he sought
— Svaðilfari his horse —
and Loki arranged
that the right be granted.
With winter's start
the work was begun.

The stallion's work
startled the gods;
he steadily hauled
the heavy stones
— always at night —
and every day
the builder labored
to lay the wall.

Fast proceeded
the fort's assembly;
by summer's start
it would stand complete.

The Aesir assembled
on seats of judgement
to moot on their doom
and deem a response.

It was soon decided
that the son of Laufey
should bear the blame
for the blight approaching.
Thus Loki must manage
that the mason forfeit,
or Lopt would lose
his life for failing.

When evening came,
out ran a mare
who neighed to distract
the stallion from work.
Away he wended
towards the mare
with the hapless builder
hurrying after.

The chase continued,
taking all night;
the stallion's running
had stopped the work.
With day's dawning
deduced the mason
that for certain his fee
forfeit would be.

The mason raged
with wrath of etins

for all to see.
The Aesir summoned
Thor from the East
to thrash the etin —
with Mjöllnir's power
he paid his wage.

But Svaðilfari had sated
himself on Loki,
and some time after,
Sleipnir was born.
Eight-footed and grey,
an awesome steed —
amongst the gods
and men the best.

## *The Duel*

For saying my tale
of single combat
at Grjóttúnagarðar,
a gift of silence
I ask from you all.
To utter my story,
I brewed my words
into Bölverk's wine.

On swift Sleipnir
had Sigföður rode;
Hrungnir he met
in the home of Etins.
Óðinn boasted
that best was Sleipnir;

Hrungnir disputed,
praising Gullfaxi.

In anger he galloped;
Óðinn he chased.
Fast he traveled
and before he knew,
the gates of the gods
he'd galloped through,
but Sleipnir was still
the swifter steed.

The Aesir bade
that burly Hrungnir
enter the hall
and have a drink.
The goblets of Thor
were given to him;
dead drunk he got,
draining each one.

With big words then
he boasted loudly:
that hall he would take
to the home of Etins.
Then he'd sink Asgard
and slay the gods
— except he'd filch
Sif and Freyja.

Only Freyja
would fetch him drink,
and all the ale
of the Aesir he'd have,

but bored of boasting,
the band of gods
then hailed to Thor
who thundered in.

He threatened Hrungnir
with hammer raised,
in spite of Óðinn's
offer of safety.
Hrungnir challenged
Hlórriði to duel
at Grjóttúnagarðar
for greater honor.

Thor accepted
the summons and spared
the unarmed etin
an honorless death,
for never before
had formal duel
been offered thus
to Eindriði.

At Grjóttúnagarðar
gathered the Etins.
To serve Hrungnir
as second in battle,
they made from clay
Mökkurkálfi —
enormously high
with heart of mare.

But Hrungnir had
a heart of stone;

of hard stone also
his head was made.
His shield and weapon
were shaped from stone;
his spleen as well
was spawned of rocks.

But prior to Thor,
Thjálfi arrived.
He advised the etin
that from underground
Véurr was advancing
to avoid his shield;
on the wheel of Hild,
Hrungnir then stood.

Water was made
by Mökkurkálfi
when furious Thor
in thunder appeared.
The clay coward
was killed by Thjálfi
with little of fight
and less of fame.

Arriving in rage,
Rym then quickly
hurled his hammer
at Hrungnir's bulk;
his whetstone-weapon
he whirled in return,
but through the hone
the hammer smashed.

The rock ruptured,
rammed by Mjöllnir;
into Hlórriði's head
then hied a shard.
The other fragment
fell to the earth
and became the world's
whetstone supply.

Into Hrungnir's head
the hammer continued
and smashed asunder
his source of thoughts.
Forward he fell,
fettering Sönnung;
firmly his feet
made fast that god.

Thjálfi and the Aesir
to Thor then came;
the limbs of the troll
they tried to lift.
But the heavy bulk
of Hrungnir's body
remained immobile
'til Magni arrived.

Though three years old,
the Ása-strength
of Jörð's grandson
— Járnsaxa's boy —
quickly lifted
those legs of stone;

he got Gullfaxi
as a gift from Thor.

Stuck in Thor's head
the stone remains,
though loosened a little
by the lays of Gróa;
By news of Aurvandil's
nearing to home
and his toe as a star,
he distracted her spells.

The stone that's stuck
still has an effect —
thus it is ill
that over the ground
you throw a hone,
for in Thor's head then
the stone is stirred,
distressing Ennilang.

Savor these sips
of sweetest mead,
and remember well
in mind this tale
of Vingþórr's victory
in valiant combat
at Grjóttúnagarðar,
the greatest of duels!

## *Freyr and Gerð*

Freyr, from Hliðskjálf,
saw the fairest of maidens:

beautiful Gerð in her garth.
He sank into sorrow,
sore with longing,
heavy with heartache for the maid.

Skírnir he sent
to score her love,
yearning for the jötunn maid.
Enticing with Draupnir,
then tempting with apples,
the messenger sought that match.

The gifts she refused,
then great was his wrath:
with self-swinging sword he menaced.
But finally with threats
of thurs-runes carved,
the maiden agreed to marriage.

Both then in tryst
at Barri were wedded;
Freyr and Gerð are together.
Our joyous Lord
has rejoined the world
with a heart that's whole again.

## *Gunnlaðarljóð*

Home at Hnitbjörg,
a hall in a mountain,
the daughter of Suttung dwelled.
Gorgeous Gunnlöð
was guarding his mead,
that 'gild from dwarves he gained.

Suttung savored
for himself alone
the precious and potent mead,
though that sumbel sat
unsipped by all
in a room so deep and dark.

Gunnlöð sat
on her golden stool
and dreamed of worlds all-wide.
Tales of heroes:
from travelers she heard
those stories of might and main.

She hoped that a hero
would hie for the mead
and relieve her lonely days.
Well she knew
that the wondrous brew
had a better and brighter wyrd.

By stone grinding
she was startled one day
from her bed of brooding dreams.
A hole appeared
in the hardened wall;
was it the hoped-for hero?

With bated breath,
from her bed she rose
as a serpent slithered out.
Before her eyes
its form had altered
to the Ás she knew was Óðinn!

Óðinn asked
to earn the mead
that Gunnlöð guarded there.
Her lust inflamed,
she allowed to him
her help to win that wine.

Secured it was
by crafty spells
and powerful chants and charms.
Galdor they'd need
to gain its release
and thus keep Hár from harm.

Sexual seið
and sorcery they worked,
grinding together with lust.
Nights all three
they needed to finish
the magic to ready the mead.

Their working done,
they wended then
to the cauldrons keeping the mead.
Óðinn sat
in eager suspense
on the stool of glowing gold.

Gunnlöð gave
to Gaut Óðrœrir,
then Boðn and Són to swig.
In sorrow she served
those sips of mead,
for she knew he'd not return.

Grímnir altered
to glorious eagle
and soared in searing sky,
leaving Gunnlöð
alone to grieve
for the hero she helped and loved.

## *Iðunn's Abduction*

For the ale of Óðinn
I eagerly quested;
I won that potion
and well I pour it.
Of Iðunn's abduction
I aim to tell
and her return to home
and what happened after.

Hœnir and Loki
were hiking with Óðinn
across the wastelands
and wilderness paths;
the hungry gods:
from a herd they took
and in earth oven
an ox they would cook.

But uncooked the ox
in the oven remained
when once and twice
they tested the meat.
Their supper delayed,
they sought a reason

and an eagle they heard
in the oak above.

The eagle demanded
the meat of his choice
for allowing the oven
at last to cook.
The Aesir agreed,
and the greedy eagle
ate the shoulders
and also the hams.

The eagle was attacked
by angry Loki.
He struck with a stick
but it stuck in place
against the eagle
when up it flew;
he was carried away,
crying for truce.

Loki agreed,
to gain his freedom,
to lure Iðunn
with her apples alone,
outside the walls
away from Asgard;
thus Loki at last
was released by the eagle.

Then Loki lured
lovely Iðunn
just as promised
to giant's grasp;

both old and grey
the gods became,
lacking her famous
and luscious fruit.

The Aesir accused
crafty Loki
and deemed the penalty
death or torture;
he'd search for Iðunn
to save his skin
if Freyja would share
her falcon shape.

To Thjazi's home
hastened Loki.
Laufeyson was lucky;
its lord was away.
The falcon flew
with the form of a nut,
Iðunn bespelled,
as he sped away.

The theft was discovered
when Thjazi returned;
the issue of Ölvaldi
as eagle gave chase.
The falcon flew
fast to Asgard
and reached the safety
inside its walls.

The eagle was unable
to end its flight,

its feathers singed
by sawdust's fire.
The eagle crashed
in the Aesir's court,
and quickly was slain
the sire of Skaði.

Then Skaði with weapons
wended to Asgard,
thirsting for vengeance
for Thjazi her father,
but an offer of weregild
the Aesir made,
and atonements three
she took from the gods.

First for Skaði:
to find a husband,
from the Aesir she'd choose,
but only by feet.
The fairest of feet
she figured for Baldur,
but Njörð she got,
Nóatún's lord.

Second for Skaði:
skillful Loki,
by binding his balls
to the beard of a goat,
looked to release
a laugh from her heart;
he fell in her lap
and at last it was freed.

Third for Skaði:
that in sky above
shaped into stars,
shining at night,
the eyes of Thjazi
were thrown by Óðinn —
for her fierce father,
the finest honor.

With atonements three
was Thjazi's daughter
with the ruling Regin
reconciled and joined.
Thus Skaði we honor
for skis and snow
and wild winter's
wondrous delights.

## The Mead Quest

Honor I Óðinn
by eagerly pouring
that precious and potent Mead.
How he won
that wynnful draught —
that spell I speak in verse.

Slaves all nine
were slain with greed
in lust for a worthy whetstone.
Thus Bölverk served
Baugi a summer;
he labored long and hard.

Bölverk had bargained
with Baugi for Mead;
at Hnitbjörg his hire they sought.
But flatly Suttung
refused that draught;
to a skillful scheme they turned.

Baugi with Rati
then bored through rock
and gnawed a narrow path.
The sly snake
then slithered fast
beyond his stinging stab.

Gunnlöð he met
and gained her love;
for three of nights he knew her.
The draughts he drank
and drained were three —
that mighty Mead he stole.

The eagle flew
to Asgard fast
with Suttung swiftly chasing.
An amount of Mead
as mud of eagle
for poetry poor was spilt.

But the greatest bounty
he brought to the gods —
a gift for the favored few.
Óðinn poured
that potent brew
for skalds and scholars alike.

For Man in Midgard
the Mead is real:
seek to win it yourself.
Drink well
and deeply enjoy
the portion I poured tonight!

## The Six Treasures

Bölverk's bounty
I bear tonight
and pour a portion to share.
I tell a tale
of treasures six,
owned by our awesome gods.

The beautiful locks
of alluring Sif
were sheared by mischief's maker;
Thor was wroth,
raged at Loki,
demanded he find a fix!

Then Loki wended
to the world of Dwarves;
their skill he schemed to hire.
The smiths began,
the sons of Ívaldi:
Goldlocks they gleamingly shaped.

The smiths continued,
the sons of Ívaldi:
Skíðblaðnir they skillfully shaped.
The smiths finished,

the sons of Ívaldi:
Gungnir they grimly shaped.

Then Loki wended
to wager with Brokk
against the greatness of treasures.
A swine's skin
by skillful Eitri
was forged to gleaming Gullinbursti.

Glowing gold
by gifted Eitri
was forged to dearest Draupnir.
Blazing iron
by brilliant Eitri
was forged to foe of etins,
was forged to mighty Mjöllnir.

Brokk was steady,
on bellows he stayed,
the scheme of the fly he foiled!
Treasures he took
to try in Asgard,
Aesir joining in judgement.

Óðinn and Thor,
and third was Freyr,
the gods who joined in judgement.
The given verdict,
the greatest treasure:
best was bane of etins,
best was mighty Mjöllnir!

## Thor's Visit to Geirröð

A warm welcome
I wish to have
for telling the tale
of a trip by Thor
to Geirröð's garth
and the games in the hall;
the draught of dwarves
I draw for you now.

Loki borrowed
from Lady Frigg
her falcon shape
to fly the realms;
at Geirröð's garth
a great hall was —
Lopt then landed
and looked in the window.

Geirröð ordered
they grab the bird;
Loki delayed
to the last moment
his flight to flee
that fellow's grasp
but found his feet
were firmly stuck.

The bird was bound
and brought to Geirröð;
on seeing the eyes,
an inkling he had
that a man it be.

He demanded the bird
speak in response;
speechless was Loki.

The unanswered etin
opened a chest
and brutally bound
the bird inside
for three of months
to thirst and starve.
Re-asked at last,
Loki then answered.

To ransom his life,
Loki gave oaths:
to Geirröð's garth
he'd beguile Thor,
without Mjöllnir
and mighty girdle.
Released was Loki
to lure as promised.

To Gríð's garth first
as a guest came Thor;
she gave warning
of Geirröð's wiles.
Iron gauntlets,
a girdle of might,
and Gríðarvöl
she gave as well.

To cross Vimur
then ventured Thor;
the river raged,

rising in flood
with Gjálp astride,
Geirröð's daughter.
Thor was struggling
but threw a stone.

He did not miss
the mark he aimed;
the stone then stemmed
and stopped the source.
He grasped a rowan
by river's edge;
thus it is hight
the help of Thor.

Thor and Loki
at last arrived
at Geirröð's garth
and were given lodging.
The single seat there
Sönnung did take;
toward the roof
it raised him up.

With Gríðarvöl
against the rafters
and pushing hard,
he pressed down then;
Both Gjálp and Greip
— Geirröð's daughters —
had their backs broken
for bearing the seat.

For games in the hall,
Geirröð called Thor
and threw a measure
of molten iron
at famous Véurr,
the friend of Man.
Eindriði caught
the iron with gloves.

The etin sought shelter
from an iron pillar;
but briskly Thor
flung back the lump.
It passed through the pillar,
plunged through Geirröð,
soared through the wall,
and sank in the earth.

Here in Midgard,
remember this tale
— with precious Óðrœrir
I poured it out —
for the evil of etins
on earth is lessened
by victorious Véurr's
valor in combat.

*Valhalla*

A spell of the lore
I speak to you now
by pouring Hropt's
powerful drink.

I sing of that hall
high on the Tree;
to warriors dead
'tis a welcome sight.

'Tis roofed with shields
and raftered with spears;
grand and glorious
in Glaðsheim stands
that greatest hall
of gods and heroes
where sturdy benches
are strewn with mail.

A wolf is lurking
at the western door,
and high above
hovers an eagle.
Fish are running
in the river nearby;
mistletoe's in the west,
a mite of a tree.

The leaves are eaten
from Lærað by Heiðrún;
mead from her udders
is the Einherjar's drink.
The limbs are eaten
from Lærað by Eikþyrnir;
dew from his horns
drops into Hvergelmir.

The gate Valgrind
is guarding the doors:

five of hundreds
and forty more.
The Einherjar go,
eight hundred per door,
on the day of doom
for deadly battle.

In the kettle Eldhrímnir,
the cook Andhrímnir
seethes Sæhrímnir,
that succulent pork.
The Einherjar eat
that excellent fare,
but the food of Vegtam
is fed to his wolves.

The wise one lives
on wine alone;
his ravens fly,
roaming the world.
The Valkyries serve
Victory-Father
and after the battles
the Einherjar's feasting.

Bragi relates
lore to Aegir;
swords shimmering
are the source of light.
Sigmund and Sinfjötli
receive the guests;
from fields of battle,
fresh they arrive.

Hrungnir challenged
Hlórriði to duel;
he dared to boast,
drunk in that hall.
Glasir gleaming
with golden leaf
is standing in front
of the famous stead.

That hall is sought
by heroes and skalds;
both far and wide
its fame has spread.
Standing strongest,
that stead is best:
it is Óðinn's own,
awesome Valhalla!

# Chapter 3: Short Calls

*Aegir Call*

Hail Aegir,
the Aesir's brewer:
in your hall you hosted the gods.
The drink you brewed
in that deep cauldron
served itself at the feast.
Son of Fornjót,
fare to our stead:
we host you here today.
Hear our call
and come today:
bring us the best of ales.

*Aegir's Daughters Call*

Hail the daughters
of Hlér and Rán,
the waves on widest oceans!
Hrönn and Hefring
and Himinglæva,
Bylgja and Blóðughadda,
Dröfn and Kólga,
and Dúfa and Uð,
seek now our holy hearth.
Hear our call
and come today:
fill us with ocean's awe.

## *Aesir Call*

Hail the Aesir,
you awesome tribe
of mighty gods and goddesses.
Sovereign main
and soldiers' might
your bring to Midgard's Men.
Riding right,
to our realm journey
from Asgard's strong estate.
Hear our call
and come today:
bring us life and light!

## *Álfar Call*

Hail the Álfar,
at home in the air,
you spirits of honored ancestors.
With beauty greater
than the glorious sun,
you are the Aesir's fairest friends.
Soar through sky,
soar through the clouds,
and stream to our stead in frith.
Hear our call
and come today:
bring us your loftiest light.

## Ancestors Call

Hail the Ancestors,
you holy ancients
and Folk of former days.
Kept in our memories,
your might lives on,
ever a boon and blessing.
From realms beyond,
arrive at our garth,
coming across the veil.
Hear our call
and come today:
join your kin with joy.

## Ask and Embla Call

Hail Ask,
and hail Embla,
you eldest ancestors of Man!
In gifts from the gods,
you gained the wyrd
that continues to work for weal.
From ancestral realms,
seek now our stead
for the blessing we brightly offer.
Hear our call
and come today:
join our joyful gathering.

## Auðumbla Call

Hail Auðumbla,
the ancient cow
who fed the infamous Ymir.
You birthed Búri
from blocks of rime
by licking three days long.
From a world forgotten,
wander to our stead,
O best and eldest bovine.
Hear our call
and come today:
bring us the milk of memories.

## Baldur Call

Hail Baldur,
beautiful god,
whose light has lifted our spirits!
In Hringhorn swift,
hie to our stead
from Breiðablik pure and bright.
Son of Frigg,
son of Óðinn,
and father to Forseti the Just,
hear our call
and come today:
wend to our wynnful garth!

## Bestla Call

Hail Bestla,
holy mother
to Óðinn, Vili, and Vé.
O bride of Borr
and Bölþorn's daughter
in the time of ancient Ymir,
from realms forgotten
ride to our stead,
you elder mother we honor.
Hear our call
and come today:
tell us the tales of old.

## Borr Call

Hail Borr,
to Bestla wedded
when everywhere Ymir ruled.
The greatest gods
you gained as sons:
Óðinn, Vili, and Vé.
From realms forgotten
ride to our stead,
you elder father we honor.
Hear our call
and come today:
speak us the spells of old.

## Bragi Call

Hail Bragi,
O brilliant skald
and husband to Iðunn of apples.
Son of Óðinn
and sire of poetry,
your staves and stanzas shine.
Ride to our stead
with runes on your tongue
and speak a spell in verse.
Hear our call
and come today:
bring us a bounty of song.

## Brokk and Eitri Call

Hail Brokk,
and hail Eitri,
you smiths unmatched in might!
Your gleaming boar
and golden ring
and iron hammer we honor!
Avoid the sun
and sneak to us here
as we praise your precious work.
Hear our call
and come today:
teach us your keenest craft.

## *Búri Call*

Hail Búri,
born from the ice
freed by ancient Auðumbla.
You were first of gods
and father to Borr
and grandfather to glorious Óðinn.
From a stead unknown,
stride to our hearth,
you eldest god we honor.
Hear our call
and come today:
teach us of elder times.

## *Dag Call*

Hail Dag,
Delling's son,
you bringer of welcome bright.
Son of Nótt
and sib of Jörð,
we crave the gift your give.
Drive onward
with doughty Skinfaxi
as you ever circle the earth.
Hear our call
and heal the world
with the spirited lift of light.

## *Dísir Call*

Hail the Dísir,
the holy mothers
of our noble kindred clans.
For the wyrd you made
that works in our lives,
as ancestors we honor you now.
We welcome you here;
wend to our stead
as you watch and ward our hearth.
Hear our call
and come today:
join your kith and kin!

## *Dvergar Call*

Hail the Dvergar
in Dark-Elf home,
you makers of mighty treasures.
With gleaming gold
and glowing iron,
your skill is best and brightest.
Burrow through rock
to be with us now
but avoid the searing sun.
Hear our call
and come today:
bring us your keenest craft.

## *Einherjar Call*

Hail the Einherjar
in Óðinn's hall
who fight and feast all day!
The Valkyrjur bear
the brightest mead
for you chosen champions to drink.
From battle's sport,
spare a moment,
and stride to our stead in glory.
Hear our call
and come today:
bring us wode and wonder.

## *Eir Call*

Hail Eir,
helpful Ásynja
and valiant valkyrie of Óðinn.
You bring healing,
O best of doctors,
and are a norn who's shaped our need.
From Hill of Healing,
head to our stead
and cure the ails of kin.
Hear our call
and come today:
bring us your healing hands.

## *Forseti Call*

Hail Forseti,
the famous son
of brightest Baldur and Nanna!
God of justice,
gentle and fair,
by you we're rightly reconciled.
Queller of quarrels,
quickly to our stead
from gleaming Glitnir fare.
Hear our call
and come today:
join us with truth and justice.

## *Freyja Call*

Hail Freyja,
O famous Lady
and wisest woman of seið.
On fair Fólkvang
is found your hall:
Sessrúmnir seats your host.
Drive your cart
that's drawn by cats
and ride to our rightful gathering.
Hear our call
and come today:
join us in fun and frolic.

## Freyr Call

Hail Freyr,
O famous Lord
and mighty Ing of Álfheim.
Fare to our stead
with fairest winds
 in Skíðblaðnir skimming the waves.
Lord of elves
and lord of frith,
ruler of rain and sunshine,
hear our call
and come today:
join us in peace and plenty.

## Frigg Call

Hail Frigg,
famous queen
and mother of Baldur the bright.
Wife of Óðinn,
wise with prophecy,
you keep your sooth in silence.
Fly from Fensalir
in your falcon shape,
and fare to our holy hearth.
Hear our call
and come today:
join us with grace and glory.

## Frigg's Handmaidens Call

Hail the handmaidens
of holy Frigg,
those loyal Ásynjur ladies!
O Sjöfn and Snotra
and Sýn and Gná,
also Eir and Fulla,
and Vár and Hlín
and Vör and Lofn,
seek now our holy hearth.
Hear our call
and come today:
join our joyful gathering.

## Gefjon Call

Hail Gefjon,
Gylfi's opponent,
who plowed from Sweden Sjælland.
With oxen sons
your awesome work
was done in a day and night.
Goddess of plowing,
gift us some time
and journey to our joyful stead.
Hear our call
and come today:
bring us clever craft.

## *Gerð Call*

Hail Gerð,
the holy wife
to fruitful Freyr of the gods.
Daughter of Gymir,
daughter of Aurboða,
at Barri your marriage was made.
From the home of the gods,
hasten to our stead,
mother of frithful Fjölnir.
Hear our call
and come today:
bring us grith and goodness.

## *Gríð Call*

Hail Gríð,
to Gaut a mistress
and mother to valiant Víðarr.
Gloves and Gríðarvöl
you gifted to Thor
to save him from Geirröð's snares.
From realm of Etins,
ride to our stead,
you thoughtful ally of the Aesir.
Hear our call
and come today:
bring us frithful friendship.

## *Gunnlöð Call*

Hail Gunnlöð,
you guarded the Mead
that Suttung snatched from dwarves.
You gave Óðrœrir
as a gift to Óðinn
for the nights you laid in lust.
From Hnitbjörg's dark
to our hearth journey,
and seek our blessing for solace.
Hear our call
and come today:
join our joyful gathering.

## *Heimdall Call*

Hail Heimdall,
Heaven's Warder,
by nine of mothers nurtured.
You roamed the world,
O whitest of gods,
and as Ríg you fathered the Folk.
From high Himinbjörg
head to our stead;
on Gulltopp gallop swiftly.
Hear our call
and come today:
watch and ward our hearth.

## Heimdall's Mothers Call

Hail the mothers
of Heimdall the white:
you bore him at the edge of the earth!
O Gjálp and Atla
and Greip and Eistla,
with Ulfrún and Eyrgjafa as well,
and Imð and Angeyja
and also Járnsaxa,
seek now our holy hearth.
Hear our call
and come today:
join our joyful gathering.

## Hel Call

Hail Hel,
holder of the dead,
that host in your hospitality.
Our forebears you keep;
they feast in Éljúðnir.
We ask that you honor them well.
Daughter of Loki,
daughter of Angrboða,
look to our living stead.
Hear our call
and come today:
bring us a blessing of remembrance.

## *Helgi Call*

Hail Helgi,
Hunding's bane,
the brave one twice reborn.
Borghild's son,
you were bound to your fetch
through deeds in life and death.
From Valhöll's realm,
ride with your valkyrie
and journey to our joyful stead.
Hear our call
and come today:
bring us noble bearing.

## *Hermóð Call*

Hail Hermóð,
you hastened to ride
for rescuing brightest Baldur.
You rode Sleipnir
to reach Hel's gate,
crossing gold-covered Gjöll.
On a swift horse ride
and seek our stead,
galloping from Asgard's gates.
Hear our call
and come today:
bring us speed for a spell.

## *Höð Call*

Hail Höð,
Hermóð's brother
and blindest son of Báleyg.
After Ragnarök,
you'll be reconciled
at last with brightest Baldur.
From the gods' garth come
by the guide of our sounds
and seek our happy hearth.
Hear our call
and come today:
bring us settlement with sibs.

## *Hœnir Call*

Hail Hœnir,
Hropt's companion
and with Mímir's memory an advisor.
Wode you gave
to wood made human;
on that shore you shaped our wyrd.
The wood of lots
one day you'll handle,
but stride to our stead for now.
Hear our call
and come today:
bring us brilliant thoughts.

## Honored Dead Call

Hail to all
the Honored Dead
who've left the world of the living.
Your might lives on,
and in memory you dwell
in a well beneath that Wood.
Lighten your spirits
and speed to our land
and bring your glory to our garth.
Hear our call
and come today:
a gift for a gift we offer.

## Iðunn Call

Hail Iðunn,
you're always young,
keeping those apples for the Aesir.
Wife of Bragi,
that wise poet,
your beauty brightens our lives.
Fare from your orchard
with that awesome fruit;
bring us a bite to taste.
Hear our call
and come today:
join us in fruitful feasting.

## Ívaldi's Sons Call

Hail to those smiths,
the sons of Ívaldi,
who made the mighty treasures!
Your hair of gold
and greatest ship
and unequaled spear we honor!
Dodge the daylight
and drive to us here
as we praise your precious work.
Hear our call
and come today:
teach us your excellent art.

## Jörð Call

Hail Jörð,
the holy earth
and mother of mighty Thor.
Rival of Frigg
and Rind as well,
the quick require your blessings.
Daughter of Nótt,
daughter of Annarr,
may we keep you healthy and whole.
For the bounty you give,
we greet you today:
hear our holy call!

## Kvasir Call

Hail Kvasir,
O keeper of wisdom
that you eagerly shared with all.
From shared spittle
you were shaped by the gods
as a truce for the warring tribes.
Your precious blood
was brewed with honey
and poured as the poetry we seek.
Hear our call
and come today:
bring your blood to our mead!

## Landvættir Call

Hail the Landvættir,
the holy spirits
who ward both land and life.
You roam and rest
in rocks and trees
and live on might and main.
From forest and field,
fare to our stead;
arrive at our garth in grith.
Hear our call
and come today:
share in our blessing's bounty.

*Lóðurr Call*

> Hail Lóðurr,
> holy life-giver
> from the doom-filled elder days.
> Blood you gave
> and bright good looks
> to the humans worked from wood.
> Friend of Óðinn,
> friend of Hœnir,
> stride to our holy strand.
> Hear our call
> and come today:
> renew the gifts you gave.

*Loki Call*

> Hail Loki,
> Lopt of the gods
> and brother of blood to Óðinn;
> maker of mischief
> and mother of Sleipnir,
> by cunning and craft you thrive.
> Son of Laufey,
> son of Farbauti,
> and friend to thunderous Thor,
> hear our call
> and come today:
> with laughter lift our spirits.

## *Máni Call*

Hail Máni,
you mighty orb;
shine on our holy hearth!
Brother of Sunna,
son of Mundilfari,
hasten away from Hati.
Your shining light
shimmers brightly;
both might and main you give.
Your silver light
lifts our spirits;
hear our holy call!

## *Mímir Call (God)*

Hail Mímir,
the mighty Ás,
whose advice is wise and welcome.
Goodly counsel
you gave to Hœnir
until your head was hewn.
Secrets you tell
to Sigtýr now,
but pause to speak us a spell.
Hear our call
and come today:
let us hear your hidden wisdom.

## *Mímir Call (Etin)*

Hail Mímir,
the mighty etin,
who wards the famous well.
Under Yew's root,
in Jötunheim,
with Gjallarhorn you get your drink.
From watching the well,
wander a spell
and travel to our trothful stead.
Hear our call
and come today:
bring us a draught to drink.

## *Móði and Magni Call*

Hail Móði,
and hail Magni,
the sons of thunderous Thor.
Angry and strong,
awesome in might,
his hammer you'll one day wield.
Gallop to our stead;
on Gullfaxi ride
from Bilskirnir, biggest of halls.
Hear our call
and come today:
bring us might and main.

## Nanna Call

Hail Nanna,
Nep's daughter,
to Baldur the bright you're wedded.
To fairest Forseti,
you're the fortunate mother;
rightly you've raised your son.
Brightly beaming,
from Breiðablik travel
and seek our happy hearth.
Hear our call
and come today:
fill us with faith and devotion.

## Nerthus Call

Hail Nerthus,
the holy mother
who brings the blessings of peace.
An island home
in the ocean you have,
far from a world of war.
Hidden from sight,
hie to our stead
in your cart that's drawn by cows.
Hear our call
and come today:
bring us a bounty of frith.

## Njörð Call

Hail Njörð,
Nóatún's lord
and ruler of riches vast.
Father of Freyr
and Freyja as well,
the fairest of feet you have.
From ocean's strand,
to our stead journey
and spend a spell with the Folk.
Hear our call
and come today:
join us with wealth and weal.

## Nornir Call

Hail the Nornir,
you holy three
who water the World-Tree's roots:
Urð and Verðandi,
you are awesome maidens,
and Skuld the obscure is third.
From work at the Well,
wend to our stead
on the strands you string in your web.
Hear our call
and come today:
weave us a joyful wyrd.

## *Nótt Call*

Hail Nótt,
Nörvi's daughter,
you bringer of darkness deep.
Mother of Auð,
mother of Jörð,
we crave the gift you give.
Drive onward
with doughty Hrímfaxi
as your ever circle the earth.
Hear our call
and heal the world
with the rightful rest of dark.

## *Óðinn Call*

Hail Óðinn,
O highest of gods
and master of skaldic mead.
Lord of the Runes,
looking for wisdom,
you hung on that holy tree.
Ride on Sleipnir
and seek our stead;
from Glaðsheim gallop swiftly.
Hear our call
and come today:
join our joyful gathering!

## Others Call

Hail to Others,
unasked but friendly:
the wynnful wights and gods
of land and water
and the lofty air,
who come in kinship and frith.
If you wish wend here,
we welcome you now
to our happy and holy stead.
Hear our call
and come today:
join us in merry and mirth.

## Rán Call

Hail Rán,
to Hlér a wife
and mother of maidens nine.
With the coins they carry
when coming below,
the drowned at sea you receive.
From your sunken hall,
seek now our stead
beyond the realm you rule.
Hear our call
and come today,
carrying the ocean's calm.

## Rind Call

Hail Rind,
to Rögnir a mistress
and mother to valiant Váli.
Your rightly raised
and readied your son,
who avenges brightest Baldur.
From realm of Etins,
ride to our stead,
you rival to Gríð and Gunnlöð.
Hear our call
and come today:
join our joyful gathering.

## Sága Call

Hail Sága
in Sökkvabekk,
where waves are cold and crashing.
From golden cups
you gladly drink
every day with Óðinn.
For a spell with us,
speed from your sumbel
and join our drinking today.
Hear our call
and come today:
bring us merry and mirth.

## Sif Call

Hail Sif,
your hair is gold,
finely forged by dwarves.
Beautiful goddess,
your brightest hair
glows like fruitful fields.
Mother of Ull,
mother of Thrúð,
and wife to thunderous Thor,
hear our call
and come today:
bring us bountiful harvests.

## Sigyn Call

Hail Sigyn,
unswerving in loyalty,
you bear that bowl of venom.
Married to mischief,
mother of Narfi,
you endure with pride and patience.
Spare a moment
and speed to our stead
while waiting for Ragnarök.
Hear our call
and come today:
in fidelity and duty join us.

## Sigmund Call

> Hail Sigmund,
> son of Völsung,
> and father to Sinfjötli and Sigurð.
> A sword as a gift
> you gained from Óðinn,
> and you valiantly avenged your father.
> From Valhöll's realm
> ride to our stead
> for the blessing we brightly offer.
> Hear our call
> and come today:
> join our joyful gathering.

## Sigurð Call

> Hail Sigurð,
> of heroes greatest:
> Fáfnir you fearlessly slew.
> Son of Sigmund,
> son of Hjördís,
> you are famed for daring deeds.
> From Valhöll's realm
> ride to our stead
> on Grani gotten from Sleipnir.
> Hear our call
> and come today:
> bring us a bounty of courage.

## Skaði Call

Hail Skaði
of the high mountains
who's married to Nóatún's Njörð.
Thrymheim's lady
and Thjazi's daughter,
by weregild you're welded with Aesir.
With skis on snow,
skillfully travel
and journey to our joyful stead.
Hear our call
and come today:
bring us the wonders of winter.

## Sunna Call

Hail Sunna,
heaven's light,
shine on our holy hearth!
By Árvak and Alsvið
you're always drawn,
scurrying away from Sköll.
Shining beauty,
shimmering brightly,
light and life you give.
Your light we love:
it lifts our spirits.
Hear our holy call!

## Thor Call

> Hail Thor,
> holy thunderer,
> greatest in might and main!
> Your hall stands
> in the home of strength:
> Bilskirnir is biggest of all.
> Drive your goats,
> galloping onward,
> toward our holy hearth.
> Hear our call
> and come today:
> join us glad in grith.

## Thrúð Call

> Hail Thrúð,
> holy goddess
> and valkyrie in Valhöll for Óðinn.
> Daughter of Thor
> and daughter of Sif,
> you were saved by sunlight from Alvíss.
> Wend from Valhöll
> and wing to our stead,
> flying with feather cloak.
> Hear our call
> and come today:
> bear us strength and beer.

## Týr Call

Hail Týr,
hofs' chieftain
and courageous ruler of the Thing.
God of war,
you gave your hand
to firmly fetter the Wolf!
Travel from the sky,
with skill bring truth,
and swiftly seek our stead.
Hear our call
and come today:
join the Folk in justice!

## Ull Call

Hail Ull,
Ýdalir's lord:
of the gods your bow is best.
With glorious skill,
on skis you hunt,
and on bone you wend o'er waves.
Son of Sif,
sail to our stead
on the shield you ride as a ship.
Hear our call
and come today:
fare to our garth in glory.

## Váli Call

Hail Váli,
avenger of Baldur;
his slayer Höð you slew.
Son of Óðinn
and son of Rind,
a duty of death you filled.
Washed and combed,
wend to us now,
and tread to our trothful stead.
Hear our call
and come today:
guide us in victory and vengeance.

## Valkyrjur Call

Hail the Valkyrjur
in Vegtam's hall
who ride to the harvest of heroes.
You choose the slain
as champions for Óðinn;
the greatest honor he offers.
Swiftly flying
with swan feathers,
soar to our happy hearth.
Hear our call
and come today:
weave us victorious wyrd.

## Vanir Call

> Hail the Vanir,
> you virtuous tribe
> of mighty gods and goddesses!
> Peace and plenty
> and prosperous seasons
> you bring to Midgard's Men.
> Striding strong,
> to our stead journey
> from Vanaheim's fields and forests.
> Hear our call
> and come today:
> bring us health and heart!

## Vár Call

> Hail Vár,
> O vital goddess,
> the Ásynja who hears our oaths.
> You bring accord
> and bless marriages
> and perceive our secret agreements.
> While watching all,
> wend to us now,
> the men and women of Midgard.
> Hear our call
> and come today:
> hear the pledges we proffer.

## Víðarr Call

> Hail Víðarr,
> avenger of Óðinn
> and enemy of the evil Wolf.
> Son of Óðinn
> and son of Gríð,
> your mighty shoe is sure.
> Seek our stead,
> O silent god;
> from Viði venture forth.
> Hear our call
> and come today:
> join our service in silence.

## Vili and Vé Call

> Hail Vili,
> and hail Vé:
> brothers to awesome Óðinn.
> From Ymir's corpse,
> you crafted the worlds,
> setting our wyrd as well.
> From creation's work,
> wend to our stead,
> here in the Midgard you made.
> Hear our call
> and come today:
> join your joyful kin!

## Völund Call

Hail Völund,
valiant hero,
matchless in skill with metal.
You wrought on Níðuð
needful vengeance
for slavery and sinews' cutting.
From realm of heroes,
hie to our stead,
flying on the wings you fashioned.
Hear our call
and come today:
bring us clever craft!

## Zisa Call

Hail Zisa,
the happy wife
to the great and trothful Týr.
The Suebi's sacrifice
you received in the past
as a patron of victory and valor.
Sail in warship
and seek our stead;
hinder harm against it.
Hear our call
and come today:
bring us valiant victory!

# Chapter 4: Long Calls

## *Call to Óðinn*

Wassail Óðinn,
O awesome god,
join our joyful gathering!
We boast your deeds
and bid you to come:
wend to our wynnful garth!

Welcome Hangatýr,
you won the Runes
by hanging on the highest tree.
Nine of nights
you needed to give
yourself to self for gain.

Welcome Hropt,
you are wise in seið,
learned from Freyja the fair.
Death at need,
knowledge of wyrd,
and many mysteries it brings.

Welcome Sigtýr,
you saved the head
of Mímir's mighty wisdom.
You sang galdor
and smeared herbs;
it tells you many tidings.

Welcome Báleyg,
you are wisest of gods:
water from that well you drank,
guarded by Mímir,
who grimly demanded
an eye as the price you paid.

Welcome Bölverk,
you burrowed to Gunnlöð
to gain the greatest of meads!
To skillful skalds
and scholars poured,
that brew is the best of treasures!

We've gathered here
to give and share
a bounty of might and main.
Hear our calls
and come today:
join us in frith as fellows,
join us in wode and wisdom!

## Call to Freyja

Lovely Freyja,
fairest Lady,
join our joyful gathering!
We boast your names
and bid you come
to our blessing with beauty and grace.

Welcome Vanadís,
the Vanir's queen
and leading light of that tribe.

Lover's trysts
are a lusty gift
of your work in the world today.

Welcome Mardöll,
maid of the sea
and bearer of Brísingamen.
Your pride and joy
is a precious jewel:
a sign of seið and magic.

Welcome Heið,
you weathered spears
and the Aesir's fiercest fires
as Gullveig to gain
a glorious rebirth
as a shining lady of light.

Welcome Valfreyja,
victory's lady
and decider of half of the slain.
Fólkvang's warriors
are fortunate indeed
to join your joyous host.

We've gathered here
to give and share
a bounty of might and main.
Hear our calls
and come today:
join us in frith as fellows,
join us in fun and frolic!

*Call to Thor*

Thunderous Thor,
threat-destroyer,
Asgard's chosen champion,
we boast of your might
and bounty of main
in the call we declare today.

At Grjótúnagarðar
in the greatest of duels,
heavy Hrungnir you slew.
Glorious honor
you gained that day,
strengthening the Gods' establishment.

A serpent you challenged
and smote with your hammer
while fishing in far-off waters.
In farthest future,
you'll fight again
and sunder that snake at last.

With molten iron
you offed Geirröð
in that brutal play of battle.
Thrym you thrashed,
that thoughtless etin
who dared to hoist your hammer.

Famed among gods,
your family is honored
by your deeds and doings of might:
Sif your wife,

and your sons and daughter,
Móði, Magni, and Thrúð.

Your hall stands
in the home of strength:
Bilskirnir is biggest of all.
With Tooth-Gnasher
and Tooth-Grinder,
your chariot charges quickly.

Drive your goats,
galloping onward,
and reach our holy hearth.
Hear our call
and come today:
join us in frith as fellows,
join us with might and main.

# Chapter 5: Ritual Dramas

## *The Abduction of Iðunn*

*Roles*
Narrator: 15 stanzas
Loki: 6.5 stanzas
Óðinn: 5 stanzas
Eagle/Thjazi: 3 stanzas
Skaði: 2 stanzas
Hœnir: 1.5 stanzas
Iðunn: 1.5 stanzas
Freyja: 1 stanza
Njörð: 0.5 stanzas

*Narrator:*
"Hœnir and Loki
were hiking with Óðinn
across the wastelands
and wilderness paths;
the hungry gods,
from a herd they took,
and in earth oven
an ox they would cook."

*Loki:*
"A glorious feast
of this great hoofed beast
will help to ease our hunger."

*Narrator:*
"But uncooked the ox
in the oven remained

when once and twice
they tested the meat.
With their supper delayed,
they sought a reason,
and an eagle they heard
in the oak above."

*Óðinn:*
"For what rhyme or reason
is the roast delayed?
I suspect an evil spell."

*Eagle:*
"I am the cause
of the cooking's delay:
alone I bear the blame.
Graciously grant
my goodly fill,
and the ox in the oven will cook."

*Hœnir:*
"Let others decide
the action we take
in the matter of eagle and ox."

*Loki:*
"To hasten our supper
I say we hearken
to the eagle's offer now."

*Óðinn:*
"And well we should,
though wary I be
of this eagle looming and large.
We'll take, eagle,

the terms you offer;
now have your fill of food."

*Eagle:*
"I'll eat my fill
of ox-flesh now;
mind not what I munch."

*Narrator:*
"On the oven to eat
the eagle sat down;
he ate the shoulders
and eagerly the hams."

*Loki:*
"That's much too much
you miserable brat;
for pride I'll make you pay!"

*Narrator:*
"The eagle was attacked
by angry Loki;
he struck with a stick
but it stuck in place
against the eagle
when up it flew.
He was carried away,
crying for truce."

*Loki:*
"Let me go,
you greedy monster;
just say what you want!"

*Eagle:*
"With her apples,
bring Iðunn alone
outside of Asgard's walls."

*Loki:*
"Alright, alright!
I really will do it!
Please now put me down!"

*Narrator:*
"Thus Loki at last
was released by the eagle,
and back he went
to the band of gods.
The travelers three
returned to Asgard
with nothing else
of note to say.
Loki went then
to lovely Iðunn;
his oath to the eagle
he'd aim to keep."

*Loki:*
"Lady Iðunn,
come look at the apples
I've found in a special forest;
The best that you bear,
bring to compare;
you'll like these luscious fruits."

*Iðunn:*
"I shall see

these sweet new apples;
Loki, lead me onward."

*Narrator:*
"Once she was outside
the walls of Asgard,
from Thrymheim came
Thjazi as eagle."

*Thjazi:*
"Hello Iðunn,
I have you now!
Your apples will feed this eagle!"

*Iðunn:*
"Help me Lopt!
Help me Loki!
Someone save me please!"

*Narrator:*
"Away to Thrymheim,
Thjazi took her;
But grey and old
the gods became,
lacking her famous
and luscious fruit.
The great Aesir
then gathered for moot."

*Óðinn:*
"Iðunn is gone
and the apples as well,
for she kept our old-age cure.
Where was last

the wife of Bragi
seen with Ás or Elf?"

*Hœnir:*
"She left with Loki,
the last I saw,
going outside of Asgard;
But why it mattered
I remembered not,
though hard I thought and thought."

*Óðinn:*
"Let mischief's maker
to this moot be brought;
Loki must answer to us."

*Narrator:*
"Loki in chains
was led to the moot
and terribly threatened
with torture or death. . ."

*Loki:*
"Please, I beg you!
I promise I'll find her,
whatever the price or pain!
Etin-home I'll search,
and all I need
is the falcon shape of Freyja."

*Freyja:*
"If of finest gold
were my falcon shape,
still to Loki I'd lend it.
Hurry fast,

and fly in search
of Iðunn and old-age cure."

*Narrator:*
"As falcon he flew,
fast to Thrymheim;
Lopt was lucky,
its lord was away."

*Loki:*
"Hail Iðunn,
I'm here at last
to whisk you away to home.
Now hold still,
I need to charm
and shift your shape for flying,
and shift your shape for fleeing."

*Narrator:*
"The falcon then flew
with the form of a nut
— Iðunn bespelled —
as he sped away.
The theft was discovered
when Thjazi returned;
the issue of Ölvaldi
as eagle gave chase."

*Thjazi:*
"What happened?
Where's Iðunn?
Loki will pay with his life!"

*Narrator:*
"But the falcon flew

fast to Asgard
and reached the safety
inside its walls.
Then the Aesir set
a sawdust blaze,
but the eagle was unable
to end its flight.
With feathers burned,
in the fort it crashed,
and quickly slain
was the sire of Skaði.
The gods and Lopt
then gathered around
the precious cargo
he placed before them."

*Loki:*
"A charm I speak
to change you back,
from nut to goddess again,
from nut to Iðunn anew."

*Iðunn:*
"Eat my apples,
Asgard dwellers:
regain your glorious youth,
regain your vital vigor."

*Narrator:*
"Finally refreshed
and full of youth,
the gods were happy
and again carefree,
'til Skaði with weapons

wended to Asgard,
thirsting for vengeance
for Thjazi her father."

*Skaði:*
"Gods of Asgard,
my grievance you'll hear —
I seek to avenge my sire.
Let the bane of Thjazi
in battle face me;
he will pay the price in blood."

*Óðinn:*
"Let us avoid
that vengeful bloodshed
and seek to settle with peace.
The Aesir now
will offer weregild —
atonements three for Thjazi."

*Narrator:*
"The gods and Skaði
agreed on the terms:
a memorial, a husband
and making her laugh."

*Óðinn:*
"Here now choose
a husband from us
by simply seeing the feet."

*Skaði:*
"I choose this one
with charming feet;
they ought to be on Baldur."

*Njörð:*
"Njörð of Nóatún
you've named as husband;
I'm happy to hear your choice."

*Skaði:*
"Now release a laugh
from my lonely heart;
I don't know how you'll do it."

*Loki:*
"I'm master of mischief
and making laughter;
with goat I'll get it done."

*Narrator:*
"He bound his balls
to the beard of that goat;
then back and forth,
both were squealing.
He fell in her lap;
finally she laughed,
and another part
of the payment was filled."

*Óðinn:*
"As final payment,
I fashion now
for your father the finest memorial."

*Narrator:*
"For Skaði's weregild,
into the sky above,
Óðinn then threw
the eyes of Thjazi,

shaped into stars
shining at night:
these bright beacons
are a brilliant tribute.
With atonements three
was Thjazi's daughter
with the ruling Regin
reconciled and joined.
Thus Skaði we honor
for skis and snow
and wild winter's
wondrous delights."

## The Creation of the Six Treasures

*Roles*
Narrator: 17.5 stanzas
Loki: 10 stanzas
Brokk: 7.5 stanzas
Eitri: 7.5 stanzas
Óðinn: 1.5 stanzas
Ívaldasynir: 1 stanza
Sif: 1 stanza
Thor: 0.5 stanzas

*Narrator:*
"Loving mischief,
Loki had cut
the golden hair
of glorious Sif.
Those strands he sheared,
no stubble remained;
that deed he did

in the dark of night.
When Sif had seen
herself next day,
she screamed and sobbed
and scurried to Thor."

*Sif:*
"Oh Thor, my Thor,
my threads of flax
have all been shaved and sheared!
Loki's scent
lingers nearby;
he must have played a part!"

*Narrator:*
"Thor went quickly
to threaten Loki
for his dastardly deed
with a doom of pain."

*Thor:*
"Her locks you sheared;
your limbs I'll smash
'til all your bones are broken!"

*Loki:*
"Spare me please!
I'll speedily fix
the hurt and harm I've caused.
I'll wend my way
to the world of Dwarves,
and hair of gold I'll get."

*Narrator:*
"The husband of Sif

harked to that offer,
allowing Loki
to leave and make good.
Down he wended
to Dark-Elf home
and entered the realm
of Ívaldi's sons."

*Loki:*
"I hail you all,
Ívaldi's sons,
and ask a favor in frith.
Make good with the gods
and grant their request
for treasures finely forged:
Golden hair,
the greatest of ships,
and for Hropt a special spear."

*Ívaldasynir:*
"We'll gift the gods
to regain their favor,
by making the treasures tasked.
Our work is best
and one-of-a-kind;
far and wide it's famed."

*Narrator:*
"The smiths began,
the sons of Ívaldi:
from gold they wrought
the gleaming hairs.
The smiths continued,
the sons of Ívaldi:

they shaped with skill
the ship Skíðblaðnir.
The smiths finished,
the sons of Ívaldi:
grim was Gungnir,
the gar they forged."

*Loki:*
"Well you've worked
these wonderful treasures;
they'll greatly please the Powers."

*Narrator:*
"Loki then left,
but lingered in Dwarf-home.
To the abode of Brokk
he brought the treasures."

*Loki:*
"Hail Brokk, old chap,
be awed by the works
of Ívaldi's excellent sons,
since Eitri can't make
anything finer,
no matter the might he bears."

*Brokk:*
"You're surely wrong
on his shining craft
that's unsurpassed and peerless."

*Loki:*
"Let's settle this now
through a serious wager
and gamble our heads on gifts.

Let the Aesir judge:
Óðinn jointly
with Thor, and Freyr as third."

*Brokk:*
"I'll take those terms.
His treasures will win,
and your head from neck be hewn."

*Narrator:*
"Eager to off
the issue of Laufey,
those two brothers,
Brokk and Eitri,
began their works
of greatest craft;
the forge was kindled,
fiercely burning."

*Eitri:*
"Brokk, my brother,
now blow steady,
as I bear this boar-skin to forge.
Continue on
until I have ended,
and out I've pulled that pig."

*Narrator:*
"When Eitri went off
to create the treasure,
a fly appeared,
flitting about.
Onto his arm
it angled and bit,

but Brokk persisted,
blowing steadily.
The skin of swine
was skillfully forged
to a boar with bristles
of brightest gold."

*Eitri:*
"Well done, brother,
is your work on the bellows;
with skill I've surely shaped.
The finest of boars
I've brought from the forge;
this gift is fit for Freyr.
Brokk my brother,
now blow steady;
to the forge I go with gold.
Continue on
until I have ended
and out I've taken the treasure."

*Narrator:*
"When Eitri went off
to create the treasure,
the fly returned,
flitting about.
On his neck it landed
and nibbled harder.
but Brokk persisted,
blowing steadily.
With greater skill
that gold was forged
into a glorious ring
by the gifted smith."

*Eitri:*
"Well done, brother,
is your work on the bellows;
with skill I've surely shaped.
A golden ring
I've gained from the forge;
this gift will honor Óðinn.
Brokk, my brother,
now blow steady;
to the forge I'm off with iron.
Continue on
until I have ended,
and out I've taken my triumph.
Greatest of all
this gift can be,
but bad if the blowing fails."

*Narrator:*
"When Eitri went off
to create the treasure,
the fly returned,
flitting about.
Onto his eyelids
it angled and bit,
'til blood was flowing
and blinded his eyes.
When the bellows came down,
he brushed at the fly
as quick as he could
to cast it away.
With awesome skill
that iron was forged
into a mighty hammer
by the matchless smith."

*Eitri:*
"Good gods, brother,
my greatest work
was nearly wrecked and ruined.
But here it is,
a hammer of might
for famous thundering Thor.
Take the treasures
to test in Asgard
and seek to win the wager.
The head of Loki
will hang on our wall;
soon we'll see his end!"

*Narrator:*
"Brokk with treasures
travelled to Asgard;
Loki likewise
landed therein.
To decide the wager,
their seats they took:
Óðinn and Thor
and third was Freyr."

*Loki:*
"Hail Óðinn,
this awesome spear
is hight Gungnir grim!
In thrust it serves
as a thane unfailing:
it'll never stop or stall.
Hail Thor,
this hair of gold
for Sif will serve as her own.

It will hold down roots
when on head it's placed
and grow as good as any.
Hail Freyr,
this finest of ships
for skimming waves is Skíðblaðnir.
It has fairest winds
— if unfurled are the sails —
always wherever it goes.
When faring's finished,
it can fold like cloth
and in pocket be kept and carried."

*Brokk:*
"Hail Óðinn,
this heavy ring
of gleaming gold is Draupnir.
Eight more of rings,
equally heavy,
it drips each nine of nights.
Hail Freyr,
this finest of boars
can cross the air and ocean
in day or dusk
or dreary night
faster than stallion or steed.
It's never too dark
in night or dark-world
for the light that beams from its bristles.
Hail Thor,
this hammer of thunder
is mighty Mjöllnir hight!
You may strike as strongly
— at your strived-for target —

and as heavy as you happen to like.
It will never fail,
and it will never miss,
and never will it fly so far
that it not come back
in needful time,
seeking its home in your hand.
And if you like,
so little it is,
that it sits inside your shirt.
The one flaw
in this finest work
is the handle's lack of length."

*Narrator:*
"The gathered gods
together decided,
and Óðinn delivered
the Aesir's judgement."

*Óðinn:*
"We've decided this contest
and settled the matter:
the dwarf has won the wager.
For guarding against
the grim frost-giants,
best is bane of etins,
best is mighty Mjöllnir."

*Loki:*
"I'll graciously give
'gild at your judgement
to redeem my dearest head."

*Brokk:*
"Your head I'll hew
with no hope of redemption;
I allow no further delay."

*Loki:*
"Catch me then!
I'm quick on my feet,
you slothful tiny twit!"

*Narrator:*
"Brokk then bounded
to bag the trickster,
but Loki leapt
and left his sight,
spiriting away
with those speedy shoes
that over both air
and ocean can run.
He called on Thor
to catch the thief
who absconded with
the skull he'd won.
Bringing him back,
Björn caught Loki,
handing him over
to the happy dwarf."

*Loki:*
"My head you've won,
but handle with care,
for none of my neck is yours."

*Óðinn:*
"His rede is right
and reckoned well;
don't harm or hurt his neck."

*Narrator:*
"Brokk took a blade
to break some holes
in Loki's lips
to loop them together,
to thread them fast
with a thong of leather.
The blade was blunted;
no bite it made."

*Brokk:*
"Better this would be
with my brother Awl;
easily he'd pierce this prat."

*Narrator:*
"As soon as he said
his sibling's name,
the awl appeared
and pieced the lips.
He tacked them tightly
and tore the edges;
the strap he stitched
is strong Vartari.
The entire tale
we've told at last:
of how Sif's hair
is hight now gold,
of the gods' gaining

their greatest treasures,
and of locking the lips
on Loki shut."

## The Winning of the Mead

*Roles*
Narrator: 12 stanzas
Óðinn: 5 stanzas
Baugi: 4 stanzas
Gunnlöð: 2 stanzas
Thralls: 1.5 stanzas
Suttung: 1 stanza

*Narrator:*
"Out went Óðinn
to Etin-realm.
Thralls nine mowed hay;
thither he came."

*Óðinn:*
"Shall I sharpen
your shearing blades?
Better by far they'll bite."

*Thralls:*
"Our work is hard;
we welcome your help.
Make sharp our biting blades."

*Narrator:*
"Our hero then took
a hone from his belt:

the scythes he sharpened,
and the slaves were pleased."

*Thralls:*
"Your strange stone
has struck quite well;
thanks for bettering these blades.
We must purchase
this prized whetstone;
now just name your price."

*Óðinn:*
"Whoever would own it
should offer me now
a reasonable price to pay."

*Narrator:*
"But all the thralls
eagerly wanted it.
Up in the air,
Óðinn threw it.
Clamoring to catch it,
they cut their throats,
shearing their necks
with sharpened scythes.
From Baugi the etin,
brother of Suttung,
Óðinn then sought
an evening's stay."

*Baugi:*
"A fix I'm in:
my fortunes are bad.
Where can I look for labor?

My slaves all nine
have slashed their necks;
my hope of harvest is gone."

*Óðinn:*
"Hail Baugi,
Bölverk's my name.
For your slaves I'll stand in stead.
A single sip
of Suttung's Mead
I'll take as my wage for the work."

*Baugi:*
"Suttung savors
for himself alone
that precious and potent Mead.
I get no say
in giving that sumbel,
but I'll try to obtain that pay."

*Narrator:*
"Thus Bölverk served
Baugi that summer;
he labored long,
lusting for Mead.
When winter came,
he wanted his hire;
thus both set off
to bargain with Suttung."

*Baugi:*
"Hail Suttung,
son of Gilling,
a favor I ask in frith.

Pour for Bölverk
a portion of Mead
as wage for summer's work.
Here in your hall,
help your brother;
that gift would demand a gift."

*Suttung:*
"Certainly not,
simply never!
No one may sip my sumbel!
Leave at once,
and look elsewhere
to find your hireling's fee!"

*Narrator:*
"Suttung sent them
sulking away.
But Bölverk said
that Baugi should try
with schemes and tricks
to score the Mead.
Baugi agreed
and began at once."

*Óðinn:*
"This auger is Rati;
I ask that you bore
a hole in Hnitbjörg now."

*Narrator:*
"Baugi then bored
and broke through stone,

and after a stint
he stopped the cutting."

*Baugi:*
"The cutting is done:
I've cleared a hole.
Now do what you will."

*Narrator:*
"But Bölverk then
blew into the hole,
and back the bits
bounced in his face."

*Óðinn:*
"The chore's undone:
you're cheating your duty.
Now bore the rest of the rock."

*Narrator:*
"Then Baugi again
bored the mountain,
and when Bölverk blew,
the bits flew in."

*Óðinn:*
"Your duty's done:
I deem that you go.
I shift my shape to sneak,
I shift my shape to snake."

*Narrator:*
"He became a snake
and crawled in the hole.
Then Baugi stabbed,

bearing the auger;
he missed his mark
from moving too slow.
Bölverk then met
beautiful Gunnlöð."

*Gunnlöð:*
"Hail you guest!
I'm hight Gunnlöð;
say now your name to me."

*Óðinn:*
"I'm Ása-Óðinn
and offer to you
three night's pleasure and play.
I ask only
to earn in return
three drinks of mighty Mead."

*Gunnlöð:*
"Welcome Óðinn!
Let's wend to bed
and share our skills with skin.
Long I've awaited
a lordly hero
who could merit this idle Mead."

*Narrator:*
"After three nights
of thrilling passion,
she brought Bölverk
to the bounty of Mead.
The three cauldrons
— in three large gulps —

he emptied at once
for all the Mead."

*Gunnlöð:*
"Óðinn my dear,
if only you'd stay
and make a home of Hnitbjörg."

*Óðinn:*
"My dear Gunnlöð,
I do what I must.
I shift my shape to soar,
I shift my shape to eagle."

*Narrator:*
"An eagle he became,
and up he flew,
escaping into
the sky above.
When Suttung saw
the soaring flight,
he also put on
his eagle form.
After Óðinn
the etin chased;
the Aesir saw,
and out they set
in the courtyard's clearing
their cauldrons three.
Óðinn flew over
and upchucked in them.
So close he'd been
to being caught
that an amount of Mead

as mud of eagle
for poetry poor
he piddled out.
All who want it
are able to have it.
But the great bounty
of that glorious sumbel
he brought to the Gods
and the best of Men;
thus Óðinn pours
that potent brew
for the skill of skalds
and scholars alike."

# Chapter 6: Praise Poems

## *A Tale of Wisdom's Well*

Now wisdom's way I praise
— 'tis Woden's holy road —
with mead I rightly made
from might of lore tonight.
Deeply drink — don't just sip —
this draught of main and gain
in hearing tell of Hár,
on how and why that eye!

First had Búri got Borr.
Then born was Ölvir-Forn:
from a crude corpse he made
what's called our home by skald.
Hanging high, nine nights long,
beholding runes as boons,
this gloried god went far
but glimpsed much more in store.

To get seið-skill he sought
sensuous Freyja then:
ecstasy alters luck.
Through herbs no rot perturbs
the head of Hœnir's bud:
hidden tales it unveils.
They're not enough to quaff:
he needed more of lore.

Wanting to gain he went
for wisdom to be his;

under the Ash he'd wend
by Etin-home and roam
along a root so right
to reach and then beseech
a dram from master Mím:
a mighty trip that sip!

Then grimly Gaut hailed Mím
who, grand with horn in hand,
refused the fuel he prized:
for free it would not be!
A price instead he paid,
a part most dear and near:
to have that gulp he gave
a globe of sight that night.

For gain his eye was gone;
then Gjallarhorn was borne
— deeply undimmed it beamed —
with draught so full of craft.
Crystal clear was its fire;
no clouds stained or remained
in sky of Skollvald's will:
screaming bright, yet no dream.

That member he gave Mím
is mighty still in sight:
rowning of realms unseen,
right it dwells, in the wells.
He's stirred to understand
through strength of both at length;
much wisdom deep he draws
from draught and eye of craft.

Onward ever he'll run,
aiming for more to claim
of wisdom wild and bold:
wode for his holy road!
Honor his eye and boon,
for always they recall
that feat of glory great
for Gods and Men to ken.

## *The Drápa of Battle Cry*

'Tis for Battle Cry,
the carried board,
that I've shaped this praise
with my surest craft;
my song is solid,
as suits that shield,
for now I tell
its needful tale.

The burnished boss,
brightly gleaming,
is an inner beacon
on this board of oak.
With a band of black
it's bound at the edge;
that cowhide wyrm
secures its world.

Its spiral pattern
spreads from center,
and three by three
are the thick gyrons,

arrondi-arrayed
in rightful manner;
with kindred colors
it's carefully painted.

Leading our way
as luminous circle,
*the awe of Battle Cry*
*is always beaming.*

Gold for the Gods
we graciously honor,
whose faith we foster
and firmly hold;
The gleaming glow
of the great old ways
we seek to show
to seekers sure.

Black for the Well
that bears our wyrd,
both deep and dark,
like the depths it holds.
'Tis firm and fast
like the famous virtues,
those guides to growth
and the good in life.

Green for the Tree,
glorious and bright,
that holds the homes,
hight Yggdrasil,
and green we keep
our great kindred

that learns the ways
to live as heathens.

In its bright colors
is our bold mission:
*the awe of Battle Cry
is always beaming.*

Cut and crafted
by keen Levi
of Coal Center
in cold December,
'tis a glorious gift
that will grace the Hearth
on our road ahead
of rising fortunes.

With sword it's paired
as a powerful set
to wield with honor
and ward our frith.
Our arms and armor
we'll always carry
while the World-Tree
is waxing green.

Hail to the gift,
hail to the giver,
and hail to the Hearth
for holding its trust.
May fame endure
for this fortunate oak
that's hight Battle Cry
and for the Hearth of Yggdrasil.

## A Drápa for Formal Sumbel

In quest I struggled
to quicken my words
and honor Óðinn tonight;
The drink of dwarves:
that draught I won,
and now I pour it in praise.

Hail to Óðinn,
the Aesir's lord
and greatest worker of wode.
The raven god
has roamed the worlds
and waxed in wisdom's might.

This god of heroes
is the greatest hero,
*for the best of the Aesir is Óðinn.*

He hung wounded
on that holy tree
to gain the glorious Runes;
with the price he paid
of pain and torment
were might and mystery won!

He is always seeking
to add to his wisdom,
*for the best of the Aesir is Óðinn.*

Suttung's sumbel
he sought to steal
to gain the skill of skalds;
by knowing Gunnlöð

for nights all three
were power and poetry won!

The Folk in Midgard
is fortunate indeed
to share in those greatest of gains;
for winning the Runes
and winning the Mead,
hail to the heroes' god,
hail to awesome Óðinn!

Now I turn
my needful praise
to the heroes in Óðinn's hall;
With mead I toast
those mighty dead
who eternally fight and feast.

Hail to the Einherjar,
the heroes of Óðinn,
those champions chosen in battle;
they feast in Valhöll
with the father of victory
on the best of boar and mead.

The cream of the Folk
is called for that host;
*the honor of the Einherjar is eternal.*

The greatest of warriors
have gained that hall
by trusting in might and main.
Their deeds and doings
of daring in battle
inspire our spirits today.

With glory in Glaðsheim,
together they dwell;
*the honor of the Einherjar is eternal.*

The greatest of skalds
have gained that hall
through pouring their mighty mead.
In the workings of Wyrd
their words live on:
the great reward for wode.

The lives they lived
are a light to heathens;
their glory is undying in death.
For showing the way
to that shining hall,
hail to the Heroes of the Folk,
hail to Óðinn's Einherjar!

To the Folk's future,
forward I look
and praise the past as well;
A full horn I raise
to the Folk today —
the modern heathen heroes.

Hail to the Folk
of heathen faith
who struggle to restore that troth!
We aim to emulate
the Einherjar well
through our mighty words and works.

Our local kindreds
labor with pride;
*the fame of our Folk is growing.*

To the chiefs and elders
who've chosen to lead
and bear that burden well,
and the heroes who work
behind the scenes —
thanks and praise I pour.

Our brilliant leaders
have blazed a trail;
*the fame of our Folk is growing.*

To the serious seekers
for their solitary work
following in Óðinn's footsteps,
who quaff the Mead
and quest for the Runes —
honor and pride I pour.

Always onward,
our efforts continue
to brighten the raven banner;
for the groundwork laid
for a glorious future,
hail to our holy might,
hail to us Heathen Folk!

## *Fólksdrápa*

Fimbultýr's bounty
I bring to the Folk

and honor also
Oðinn's nation.
His holy mead
helps our people
remember well
their mighty spirit.

Our Northern blood
is a noble blessing;
ancestral deeds
have set our doom.
Be it Germanic, Norse,
or mighty English,
through the Well of Wyrd
it works today.

They bore the Runes
and battled Rome;
they conquered lands
and combed the seas.
Through deeds and doings
of daring in the world,
their might and main
have made them famous.

Our ancient ancestors
are an awesome folk.
*Our Folk endures*
*with fame undying.*

The roots of our Folk
had run quite deep;
a vicious conversion
they survived intact.

The legacy of language
links us together
across the centuries
of cultural change.

In legend and lore,
their lives we remember
to inspire our spirits
and spur us to act.
Their values and virtues
of vital power
are the holy heritage
of heroes today.

Whether old or new,
ancient or modern:
*Our Folk endures
with fame undying.*

Our Folk today
has found its roots,
rightly raising
raven banners!
Our ancient gods
we honor again,
bringing their might
back to Midgard.

We learn the lore
and live with virtue;
we rist the Runes
and rown them anew.
We rebuild the bonds
that bind the Folk;

we make it whole
and healthy again.

Our efforts honor
the ancestors well!
*Our Folk endures
with fame undying.*

With care the Folk
secures its future
and builds a base
— a beacon of hope —
for its work to come
in a world of strife,
for the road ahead
is rough indeed.

Restoring culture
and strengthening kin
will gird our Folk
against its foes.
But act we must
and always struggle
to keep our heritage
secure and whole.

Remember well
this mead I've won
and savor the sweetness
in the sounds I've poured,
for the precious poetry
in potent words
can fortify the Folk
with Fimbultýr's might!

## *Mead for Camp Netimus*

For Camp Netimus
and its caring staff,
I make and pour
this precious mead.
In the Poconos
of Pennsylvania,
it's nestled nicely
in nature's beauty.

Hail to Netimus
and its happy staff,
ever deserving
of honor and praise.
For the fine feasts here
that fill our stomachs,
us happy heathens
will hail those cooks.

From the lake below
to the lands above,
with a mighty lodge
and many cabins,
by stalwart staff
this stead is served;
whole and healthy
they hold its spirit.

Over eighty years
this awesome stead
has guided girls
through growing up.
But in the off-season

for us it is here,
and for other
East-Coast heathens.

Clean and kept well,
this camp is renowned
by the heathens here
who hold their blóts
and the friendly wights
who fill these woods;
both seen and unseen
give serious thanks.

These wonderful folk
have welcomed us!
Their hospitality
to true heathens
is a boon and blessing
that builds our Folk,
so that year after year
we yearn to return.

For hosting us here,
this hail I make
to the people I thank
with potent staves,
and this praise I finish
with powerful toasts:
Hail Camp Netimus,
and hail the cooks!

## *An Offering to Nettie*

For the mightiest wight
that wards this land,
I brewed this beer
and bear it today.
Of land wights here,
alone she is named;
on a sign somewhere,
I saw her reckoned.

Hail to Nettie,
named for her home
known as Netimus
in the Northeast realm
of Pennsylvania's
vibrant domain,
a place in the Poconos
of pride and joy!

She lives in the lake
and on land as well;
in serpent's form,
this friendly wight
burrows about,
above and below,
in the grass and trees
and ground as well.

O'er eighty years,
always watching,
neighborly Nettie
has nurtured this camp.
She's guided girls

in growing up
from the lake below
to the limits above.

Along with its staff,
this stead she serves;
whole and healthy
she holds its spirit.
In off-season also
she's always here
for the groups and guests
who go to this camp.

This winsome wight
has welcomed us!
Her hospitality
to true heathens
is a boon and blessing
that builds our Folk,
so that year after year
we yearn to return.

For welcoming us,
this wight I thank,
and all her friends
I honor as well.
My might and main
through malt I offer,
and here I pour it:
Hail to Nettie!

*Pagan Praise to Freyr*

For Pittsburgh pagans
I pour this mead,
gained from the gladsome Lady.
Gathered together
at this grithful stead,
we honor Ingvi now!

With Freyr today
his fruits we enjoy
and celebrate well the season
while peering forward
and planning the future,
for all in time must end.

Though he's fated to fall
in that future battle
— the infamous Ragnarök —
his fruits and frith
will flourish again
in the realm that's raised anew.

As well for us,
our winters will end,
followed by harvest fruits,
for life anew
is lurking always
beyond the drapes of death.

So here with pride
we praise our Lord,
that great and famous god,
the son of Njörð

and his sister-wife:
the grand and glorious Freyr.

This lord of elves
lives with the Aesir:
a union of tribes through truce.
This god of the Vanir
to Gerð is married:
a union of life and land.

All love Ing
for his excellent boons,
the peace and plenty he brings.
Wide it wanders,
his wagon of blessings,
and now we name his gifts.

For the fruitful fields
and fertile wombs
— the harvests great and good —
we gladly give
our gracious thanks
to the ruler of rain and growth.

For the pleasure and passion
that the people enjoy
— the lust and libido he brings —
we gladly give
our gracious thanks
to the master of phallic might.

For the famous frith
and fortunate weal
— the peace and luck in life —
we gladly give

our gracious thanks
to the god of rightful riches.

In mead with might,
we mix our thanks
and pour that potion to Freyr.
We strengthen the bonds
that bind us together
through a glad exchange of gifts.

Thus may he gift
our great community
for the blessing we bring in frith.
As Pittsburgh Pagans,
we give praise today!
With pride and purpose we hail,
and we hail to fruitful Freyr!

## Sumartímadrápa

This song I brewed
with sweetest honey
to celebrate summer
and sun's bright light.
I made this mead
with mirth today,
to fill the folk
with frolic and joy.

Sif and Iðunn
and Sunna we hail
for golden growth
in this greatest time.
Sweet summer is

of seasons best,
with birds and beasts
to brighten the world.

In sun and warmth,
we celebrate life;
the longer days
lift our spirits.
It is greeted as well
by the gods we honor,
for the force of life
is flowing strongest.

For the spirit of life
in this special time,
*summer and sunshine*
*we celebrate now.*

The strong sunshine
and storms of summer
will grow the crops
that grace our tables.
The harvest's bounty
is ahead for us:
from brightest light,
the best of food.

The warmth of summer
is welcomed by flowers;
bright and fragrant,
they bloom this season.
Their nourishing nectar
is needed by bees

for the honey made
into heathens' mead.

For the blessings brought
by brighter light,
*summer and sunshine
we celebrate now.*

Loaded with leaves,
the limbs of trees
provide to us
their valued shade.
To the waters we wend,
in their warmth we swim,
and we take to the roads
for travel and leisure.

For the fun and frolic
of festival days
— the things and moots —
our thanks we give.
We gather to gift
our gods outdoors
with blue sky above
our blessing-steads.

Hail to summer,
that happy season!
Enjoy the sunshine
of these joyful days,
and savor well
the sounds I poured
in the skaldic mead
I skillfully made.

## Thor Processional Chant

Great Thor, Thor, Thor,
the thunderer we hail,
that greatest son of Gaut.
We celebrate now
this son of earth
for all his great good gifts.

Ásabrag we hail,
the Aesir lord,
that greatest god of karls.
That warder of workers
gives weal unto all
where oak or rowan rises.

*For Man in Midgard*
*he's a mighty defender*
*who hallows and holds our shrines.*
*For Man in Midgard*
*he's a mainful patron*
*who furthers the fecund earth.*

Eindriði we hail,
and onward he strives
to ward the worlds 'gainst etins.
Gjálp and Greip
and Geirröð, too,
he ended to aid the worlds.

*For Man in Midgard*
*he's a mighty defender*
*who hallows and holds our shrines.*
*For Man in Midgard*

*he's a mainful patron*
*who furthers the fecund earth.*

Harðhugað we hail,
his heart is greatest:
his boldness boosts our courage.
He slew Hrungnir
to hold them safe,
the Bonds and their boons in Asgard.

*For Man in Midgard*
*he's a mighty defender*
*who hallows and holds our shrines.*
*For Man in Midgard*
*he's a mainful patron*
*who furthers the fecund earth.*

Hlórriði we hail
for the help he gives
that blesses our fertile fields.
The rain he brings
in righteous downpours,
by thunder from mighty Mjöllnir.

*For Man in Midgard*
*he's a mighty defender*
*who hallows and holds our shrines.*
*For Man in Midgard*
*he's a mainful patron*
*who furthers the fecund earth.*

Véurr we hail,
that valiant warder
of Midgard's mighty shrines.
Both barrow and vé

he blesses and holds,
hallowing the runes we write.

Hail the hallower
— that holy warder —
hail to Thor, Thor, Thor!
Hail the Great One
— that glorious Ás —
hail to Thor, Thor, Thor!

## An Ull Poem

Wulþuz and Wuldor,
as well as Ollerus:
the other names
of Ull we know.
This glorious god
is gifted with skis
and surfs the seas
on a sorcerous bone.

Oaths had Atli
— on Ull's great ring,
sworn to Gunnarr —
forsaken for gold.
The god's blessing
— glory brightest —
departed from him,
replaced by death.

In Ýdalir
is Ull's dwelling,
where winter's winds
are whirling about.

He hunts the game
that happy gods
fix for fine feasts
with fimbul guests.

This accomplished archer
is called upon
— the son of Sif —
for single combat.
Little else we know,
yet lift him a horn
and honor Ull
with excellent mead!

## Vetrartímadrápa

I stirred these staves
with strongest honey
to welcome winter
with a wassail now.
I made this mead
with mirth today
to fill the folk
with frolic and joy.

Ull and Skaði
and Óðinn we hail
for wild winter's
wondrous delights.
The winds of winter,
whipping about,
will drive the snows
in this darker time.

The life of the world
now lies in wait,
sleeping soundly
in silent rest.
For the passing away
of the prior year,
winter is greeted
by gods and men.

For the spirit of renewal
in this special time,
*winter and wassails*
*we welcome now.*

The Wild Hunt rides,
wending furiously,
with awesome Óðinn
always leading.
In the whistling wind
the unwary are caught;
in rage and wrath
that ride they join.

Inside and safe
we celebrate life
while the restless dead
are roaming the night.
The Hunt is a harvest
that harrows the land,
preparing it well
for the planting to come.

For frights outdoors
and feasts indoors,

*winter and wassails
we welcome now.*

The Yuletide days
we yearn for most:
those twelve long nights
in our troth are best.
With friends and family
we feast and celebrate,
with flowing mead
and finest meat.

The darkest of days
— when done and past —
brings us the light
we laud and praise.
We gather to gift
our gods by the fire,
warm and happy
with wassail in hand.

Hail to winter,
that hallowed season!
Enjoy the feasting
of these joyful days,
and savor well
the sounds I poured
in the skaldic mead
I skillfully made.

## *Yggdrasilsdrápa*

From trees are made
us true heathens,

and I seek silence
for singing my praise
of that tallest tree
— truly mighty —
that holds the homes
and is hight Yggdrasil.

From its drops of dew,
a draught I brew
of Ygg's ale now
and open that flow
to stir with words
our wode tonight.
Drink now deeply
this draught of skalds.

Of trees it is best
and I truly name
the nine bright worlds
that needle-ash bears.
The North has Niflheim
and its numbing Ice.
The South has Muspellsheim
and its searing Fire.

The West has Vanaheim,
the world of the Vanir.
The East has Jötunheim,
the Etins' home realm.
Above is Ljósálfheim,
the blessed realm of Elves.
Below is Svartálfheim,
the land of the Dwarves.

Highest is Asgard,
home of the Aesir.
Lowest is Hel,
the land of the Dead.
But Midgard for Man
is in the middle of all.
Now hight are the worlds
that hang on that Tree.

With worlds all nine,
that Wood does shine.
*Always that Tree*
*evergreen shall be.*

That Tree rises
from roots and wells;
three each it has,
its thirst they quench.
A root in Hvergelmir
— that roiling cauldron —
provides it the power
of primal nature.

A root in Mímisbrunn
— that Mímir watches —
stores the matter
of memory and wisdom.
A root in Urðarbrunn
— the realm of the Norns —
accumulates the wyrd
that works in the Tree.

From the wells it needs
those waters and deeds.

*Always that Tree
evergreen shall be.*

Burdened with beasts,
it bears them well.
A stately eagle
stands at the top,
Níðhögg beneath
gnaws on the roots,
and Ratatosk with gossip
runs between them.

Hungry harts four
harrow it also.
Numberless serpents
slither beneath it.
In farthest future
the fire of Surt
will burn the Tree's
trunk and branches.

That harm and thrash
hinders the Ash.
*Though trials arrive,
the Tree will survive.*

Near Urðarbrunn
the Norns do dwell.
The first is Urð
of formative past.
The second is Verðandi
of ceaseless becoming.
The third is Skuld
of threatening due.

With water and mud
they wet the Tree
to keep away
decay and rot,
and they lay layers
for life in the Well;
their faithful work
furthers that Tree.

With wyrd they heal
that Wood's ordeal.
*Though trials arrive,*
*the Tree will survive.*

But the best of burdens
it bore of old
when the Aesir's lord
— eager for wisdom —
sought the mysteries
and mounted that Steed
for nights all nine
of needful riding.

Thund was hanging
in thirst and hunger
from high branches
with harrowing wound
to gain by ordeal
a glimpse of death;
thus as gallows
the great Tree served.

The Worker of Wode
wanted the power

that was offered only
by the awesome Runes.
With a final scream
he fulfilled his quest
and lifted at last
their lore from the Tree.

Great Yggdrasil
is always green,
despite the burdens
that would break its spirit;
that source of life
and sacred lore
is ever deserving
of honor and praise.

May Elm and Ash
give ear to these words:
Outside and in,
Yggdrasil is real,
and may this mead
give might to both —
to the Tree without,
to the Tree within!

# Chapter 7: Stand-alone Sumbel Toasts

## *Aegir Toasts*

Hail to Aegir
and the ale he makes
for the gods he hosts in his hall.
For the brewer's bounty
of beer and mead,
hail to excellent Aegir!

Hail Aegir,
Hlér of the oceans
and brewer of Asgard's ale.
The best of banquets
with beer he hosts,
brewed in the biggest of kettles.
The spouse of Rán —
they spawn together
the billowing white-capped waves.
For mead brewing
and the might of the seas,
hail to Aegir the ale-smith!

## *Aesir Toast*

Hail the Aesir,
the holy powers
of the world atop the Tree.
For the light they give
that illumines our world,
hail to the excellent Aesir!

## *Ancestor Toast (General)*

Hail the ancestors
of elder times,
those famous folk and heroes.
They laid for our lives
the layers in the Well —
the might and main of orlog!
Today we do
our duty to them:
remembering well their works.
A fimbul full-horn
to those folk we raise.
Hail to our honorable ancestors!

## *Ancestor Toast (Personal)*

Hail to my ancestors,
holy and eternal,
my folk who came before.
The long departed
and lately passed,
they remain in memory and wyrd.
To Grandma Dorothy
and Grandma Margaret,
caring and kind to all.
To Aunt Delores
and Aunt Francis,
wise and well-liked by all.
To Grandpa John
and Grandpa Harvey,
who I was never fated to know.
To Uncle Louis

and Uncle Mike,
who prior to my life had past.
To others unnamed
yet always there,
and others I never knew.
For the part of my wyrd
they put in the well,
hail to my honorable ancestors!

## *Baldur Toast*

Hail Baldur,
Breiðablik's lord:
the light most loved of the gods.
Forseti's father
is famed for his goodness.
Hail to Baldur the bright!

## *Forseti Toast*

Hail Forseti
for helpful justice
and rulings right and even.
For quelling quarrels
quickly and fairly,
hail to famous Forseti!

## *Frau Holle Toast*

Hail Frau Holle
of Heidnische Folk,
that glorious goddess of the home.

For rewarding well
our weaving and spinning,
hail to mighty Holle!

## Freyja Toasts

To Freyja for freedom
and frolic I hail:
with love she lifts our spirits.
For pleasure and play
and the power of seið,
hail to fairest Freyja!

Hail Freyja,
holy Vanadís,
the bearer of Brísingamen.
To the gods she came
as Gullveig the witch,
three times burned and bloodied,
but in Hár's hall,
as Heið reborn,
she joined the gods and goddesses,
wise in the witchcraft
we welcome as seið.
Hail to fairest Freyja!

## Freyr Toasts

Hail Freyr,
famous Lord,
for harvest great and good.
For the fortune and frith

that the folk enjoy,
hail to fimbul Freyr!

Hail Freyr,
a friend to all
and lord of light and elves.
The bane of Beli
is a bringer of frith
who we honor for excellent harvest.
Gerð's husband
is gracious and kind,
that celebrated son of Njörð.
For peace and pleasure
and prosperous seasons,
hail to famous Freyr!

## Frigg Toast

Hail Frigg,
famous queen:
sooth in silence she keeps.
For the mothers she watches
and wards in spirit,
hail to highest Frigg!

## Heimdall Toast

Hail Heimdall,
Heaven's Warder,
the son of sisters nine.
With eyesight unmatched
and excellent hearing,
this guardian seldom sleeps.

For bringing back
the Brísingamen
and warding well the Bifröst,
Gullintanni
gains our praises.
Hail to watchful Heimdall!

## Iðunn Toast

Hail to Iðunn,
the apple lady
and glorious goddess of youth!
Bragi's wife
has blessed our faith
with valued youth and vigor.
For the bounty of blessings
she's brought to our troth,
I pour my praise today.
For her luscious fruit
that is life itself,
hail to helpful Iðunn!

## Óðinn Toast

Hail Óðinn,
holy Sigtýr
and lord of the awesome Aesir!
Wide he wandered
for wisdom's gain
in quests for might and main.
Glorious gifts
he gave to Men

through craft beyond our ken.
For aiding well
his earthly kin,
hail to helpful Óðinn!

## *Sunna Toast*

Hail Sunna
in heaven's realm:
with light she lifts our spirits.
For her shining might
that is sure and bright,
hail to soaring Sunna!

## *Thor Toast*

Hail Thor,
thunder's wielder,
Asgard's chosen champion!
That bane of etins
and best of warriors
is father to Móði and Magni.
He slew Hrungnir
and hammered Thrym
with peerless might and main.
For warding well
this world of Midgard,
hail to thunderous Thor!

## Týr Toast

>Hail Týr,
>the trothful god
>who fettered fast the Wolf!
>For paying the shild
>in applying that fetter,
>as a god of oaths he's honored.
>A patron of justice
>and judgement by arms,
>he sacrificed self for right.
>For frith at things
>and fairest deemings,
>hail to trusty Týr!

## Ull Toast

>Hail Ull,
>the huntsman of gods
>and best with bow of yew.
>On skis and bones
>he skillfully travels.
>Hail to the Glorious God!

## Wayfarer Toast

>Hail us heathens,
>for here we depart,
>wayfarers wending home.
>On streams of stone
>we'll steer on our ways;
>may we safe and sound arrive.

With fond memories
of our friends and kin,
hail to our holy gathering!

## *Wights Toasts*

Hail to the rest
of ready wights
here in frith as fellows:
the heathen gods
and happy spirits.
Hail to the holy others!

To the wynnful wights
that ward this land:
in frith as fellows we've come.
Our praise and thanks
we pour to you all:
Hail to the holy land-wights!

# Chapter 8: Sumbel Toast Sequences

## *A Disting Sequence*

For fertile fields,
to Freyr I hail
and for harvests great and good.
For frith with folk,
to Freyr I hail
and for peace and plenty this year.
For passage through winter
and the wooing of Gerð,
hail to fruitful Freyr!

To völur among ancestors
and their visions I hail:
in faith you served the Folk.
May your sight today
resurge in the world;
hail to visionary völur!

Hail to Disting,
for deep are my seeds
planted for greatest growth,
planted for holiest harvest:
for Freyr to make fertile
the fields of my mind,
so that I grow in wisdom and wynn,
so that I harvest words and works;
for völur's visions
to vivify my mind,
so that I read the runes aright,
so that I pour the precious mead.

For growing in might
and growing in main,
hail to furrowed fields,
hail to Holy Disting!

## *A Summerfinding Sequence*

Hail to Ostara,
the Eastern lady
and glorious spirit of spring!
Dróttning of dawn,
dear and shining:
hail to Holy Easter!

Hail to Sigurð,
Sigmund reborn,
the highest hero of the Folk!
He fearlessly slew
the serpent Fáfnir;
hail to Sigurð Sigmundarson!

Hail to my rebirth
that's bright with runes,
shining and sure in this year,
tried and true in this year.
My doom shall be
the deeds of a hero,
bright like Easter's brilliance,
famous like Sigurð's feats.
For my words and works
to wax in greatness,
hail to the spirit of spring,
hail to my rebirth in brightness!

## *A May Day Sequence*

Hail to Óðinn,
highest of Aesir,
for giving self to self.
For poetry's power
and potent runes,
hail to holy Óðinn!

Hail to that tree,
our holy ancestor,
and the worlds it brightly bears.
Of trees we were made,
but that tree was first:
Hail to Holy Yggdrasil!

Hail to the Runes
that rightly I seek:
both the bright and the murk,
both the inner and the outer.
Awesome Óðinn
I echo in my search,
hanging tree on tree,
giving self to self.
By seeking mysteries
I swell in might:
hail to the righteous Runes,
hail to my quickening Quest!

## *A Midsummer Sequence*

To the gods of the Folk
and glorious Sunna,

your lives enlighten our hearth.
To Óðinn and Týr
and awesome Baldur,
to Frigg and fruitful Iðunn,
to Thor and Freyja
and Freyr her brother,
hail to Gods and Goddesses!

To Hengest and Horsa
who harried Britain,
and Beowulf of the glorious Geats,
to Sigurð and Sinfjötli
and Sigmund their father,
those valiant heroes of Völsung,
to Bragi and Ref
and brilliant Egill,
poets who poured the mead,
and to numerous awesome
others unnamed:
Hail to the Heroes of the Folk!

Hail to us heathens,
happy and proud,
and all our holy heroes,
and all our glorious gods.
Our strong community
is standing with might,
sturdy and whole for heroes,
shining and grand for gods.
For glory we strive
and greatness we struggle,
to remember our mighty heroes
and honor our awesome gods.
For kith and kin,

and keeping together,
hail to our famous Folk,
hail to the Hearth of Yggdrasil!

## A Freyfaxi Sequence

One-handed Týr:
the Wolf he raised,
courageously feeding Fenrir.
Bravely he paid
the price to bind him.
For his hand I hail to Týr!

Hail to the Norsemen
for the holy Thing,
that gathering of folk in frith,
that joining for joy
and justice-keeping:
one of their wondrous gifts.
For hallowed custom,
helpful traditions,
honorable ancestors' wisdom,
valuable virtues,
and volumes of lore,
hail to the noble Norsemen!

Hail to the Hearth
and its holy traditions:
its Althing of rightful rulings
and its Keys of valuable virtues.
Though young in years
it yearns for greatness,
through its deeds and doings of glory,

through its honor of ancestors and gods.
At this tide we toast
to Týr and Freyr
for courage true and trustworthy,
for harvest full and fortunate.
For its life to lengthen
and last forever,
hail to our heathen kindred,
hail to the Hearth of Yggdrasil!

## *A Winterfinding Sequence*

Hail to Thor,
hearty thunderer,
greatest in might and main!
For watching well
and warding our steads,
hail to thunderous Thor!

Hail to the Dwarves
in Dark-Elf home
for the many crafts they ken.
For the might and main
they make into treasures,
hail to the industrious Dwarves!

Hail to the ancestors
for their arts and crafts
that through archaeology we know:
culture's legacy,
kept by the Dwarves.
Hail to the holy ancestors!

Hail to the Hearth
for its heathen pride
and its steady presence in Pittsburgh
and its powerful presence in the world.
For its growing reach
in the realm of Midgard,
hail to our guiding gods,
hail to the Hearth of Yggdrasil!

## A Harvest Sequence

Hail to the Vanir,
holy and virtuous,
for seasons of growth and goodness.
Hail to Freyja
and Freyr her brother;
hail to Njörð and Nerthus.
Hail to the Alcis
of elder days
and more who are lost to memory.
For the wealth and weal
to the world they bring,
hail to the wondrous Wanes!

Hail the Ynglings
by Yngvi sired,
that famous line of Fjölnir.
Glory and legends
they gained for the Swedes;
hail to the Ynglings of old!

For my wealth and weal
to wax and grow

as it did for the Ynglings of old,
as it does for the wondrous Wanes,
I honor the Ynglings
and I honor the Wanes
for my glory to greatly increase,
for my fortune and fame to grow.
I quest for goals
to quicken my glory
that the fire of fame I kindle,
that the line of legends I join.
With runes and mead
I make the road:
hail to my growing in glory,
hail to my waxing in worth!

## A Winternights Sequence

Hail to the Elf-Lord,
and hail to the Vanadís,
the Lord and Lady of the Folk!
Your warmth we welcome
as winter approaches,
that lengthy looming darkness.
King of the Álfar
and Queen of the Dísir,
you keep us hale and whole!
For frolic and frith
and fire in winter,
Hail to Freyr and Freyja!

Hail to the Álfar,
and hail to the Dísir,
the awesome ancestors of the Folk!

We welcome you here
as winter approaches;
watch and ward our stead.
Olden fathers
and olden mothers,
in memory your lives yet live.
For the wyrd you made
that works in our lives,
hail to you holy ancestors!

For my words and works
to wax in might
and honor the Lord and Lady,
and honor the Álfar and Dísir,
I seek the Runes
and rightly aim
to stain those staves within,
to stain those staves without,
and I quest to quaff
the quickening draught
to stir my wode and will,
to work as skald and scholar.
For the groundwork laid
by gods and ancestors,
hail to their helpful wyrd,
hail to my holy quests!

## *Another Winternights Sequence*

Hail to Ingvi,
the Elves' high lord,
for the gift of harvest you've given.
Elf-home you got

as a gift for teething.
Hail to awesome Ingvi!

Hail to the Álfar
in the heights of Álfheim,
those awesome fathers of the Folk!
For your frith and help
to the Folk in Midgard,
hail to you holy Elves!

Hail to our ancestors,
ancient and modern,
who've joined the Elves in the air.
We honor you now
through needful duty.
Hail to our holy ancestors!

Hail to the Hearth
as it heads into winter
for its layers of wyrd in the well,
for its folk and the frith in their lives.
The Aesir and Elves
for aid we thank:
Hail for their helpful doings,
hail to the Hearth of Yggdrasil!

## *A Fallen Heroes Sequence*

Hail Hropt,
the heroes' god:
his stead they strive to reach.
The hospitality
as host he offers
is unrivaled in all the realms.

Valhöll's lord
is a valiant hero
who calls to the few who'd follow
to ride his road
for Runes and Mead.
Hail to Óðinn for heroes!

Hail the Einherjar,
the heroes of Valhöll,
the champions chosen by Óðinn.
The mead they drink
is a mainful boon;
hail to the excellent Einherjar!

Hail the Heroes,
the highest of the Folk,
for words and works unmatched:
the fallen in war,
famed for battles
and fearless in the face of death,
and the skalds and runers
who by skill with words
spoke of their spirits in Valhöll.
For the holy wyrd
in the well they laid,
hail to the Heroes of the Folk!

## A Mothernight Sequence

Hail Frigg,
holy mother
and lady of the awesome Aesir.
In the Yuletide now,

we yearn for her might.
Hail to helpful Frigg!

Hail the Dísir,
our holy mothers
and awesome ancestors of the Folk!
We welcome you here
as winter approaches;
watch and ward our stead.
Awesome mothers
of elder times,
in memory your lives yet live.
For the wyrd you made
that works in our lives,
hail to you holy ancestors!

To the year completed
and the Jera I gained
— my learning of lore and tongues,
my victory and skills at skaldcraft,
my work and growth in the Gild —
for filling my life
with fortune and wonder,
hail to my words and works!

## A Yule Sequence

Hail Óðinn,
holy father
and lord of the excellent Aesir.
As Jólnir he rules
the Yuletide now;
hail to all-father Óðinn!

Hail the Goths,
by Gaut brought forth,
that hardy host of old.
Gold they plundered
and gained from Rome;
hail to the glorious Goths!

To the year to come
and the Jera I'll gain
— in my scholarly writing and research,
in pouring my poetry's mead,
in progress on my runic road —
for greater words
and more glorious works,
hail to my victories ahead!

## *Another Disting Sequence*

Hail Freyr
for holy frith
and the hope of harvest to come.
For peace and plenty
and the plows he charms,
hail to helpful Freyr!

Hail the Dísir,
our dear ancestors
and mighty mothers of the Folk!
They began our wyrd
and watch us now;
hail to the holy Dísir.

My mind is plowed
and prepared for growth

with skill in skaldcraft great,
with skill in scholarship great.
For a mind that's filled
with fruits to harvest,
hail to the seeds I've saved,
hail to the seeds I've sown.

## *Another Midsummer Sequence*

Hail to the Gods
and Goddesses all,
our awesome elder kin.
Their bright blessings
are a benefit here
to the men and women of Midgard.
Through words and works,
our worth we grow,
and our offerings are filled with honor;
their gifts with gifts
we gladly repay!
Hail to the Gods and Goddesses!

Hail to our ancestors
of elder times
for their mighty words and works.
That folk endured
with fame undying,
preserved in legend and lore.
Our efforts today
honor them anew
with further words and works.
For the bright blessings

in the bonds we share,
hail to our holy ancestors!

Hail to us Heathens
in the Hearth of Yggdrasil
at the height of summer sun,
as we here in sumbel celebrate!
We restore the troth
and trust in virtues,
to learn and live as heathens,
to gain and grow as heathens!
While the World-Tree
yet waxes green,
Yggdrasil's Hearth is whole,
Yggdrasil's Hearth is hale.
Ever onward,
it's always thriving —
hail its lengthening life,
hail the Hearth of Yggdrasil!

# Chapter 9: Prayers

*Aegir Prayer*

> O awesome Aegir, excellent brewer,
> with hospitality you hosted a troop
> of Aesir and Elves in your eminent hall.
> Bless our brewers with a bounty of ale
> in the admirable craft they keep with honor.
> Make us mindful of commitments to guests,
> that we wax in worth through work as hosts.
> Confer your fire on the Folk today,
> that our people prosper for the Powers' sake.

*Ancestors Prayer*

> O honored Ancestors, ancient and recent,
> we praise your deeds with pride today,
> for your lives live on in the light of memory.
> Deal us reminders of remembrance duties,
> that we gladly give our gifts to you.
> Watch well and ward your worldly offspring,
> that our Folk endures through future days.
> Inspire our spirits and spur us to act,
> so we win renown that's worthy of you.

*Baldur Prayer*

> O blameless Baldur, bright Óðinsson,
> you are gracious, loved, and glad of heart.
> May we live our lives and be loved so well,

that many will weep and miss us dearly
when we wend off to the world of death.
With purity bless us, and praise from folk,
and lead us to live so that light will shine
from our souls in joy. Save our spirits
that we live again and can leave from Hel.

## *Bragi Prayer*

O brilliant Bragi, you're the best of skalds
and wise with words. Your wealth we seek:
eloquent oratory, excellent writing,
and skill in skaldcraft. Let our skulls be filled
with these glorious gifts of great renown.
Succor our souls with your song and verse;
let our hearts be lifted with your harp's music.
With runes on your tongue, give rede to us,
that well we wax in your wisdom crafts.

## *Dag Prayer*

O dearest Dag, Dellingsson best,
the day you bring with your drive through sky,
and your rightful rhythm regulates life.
Bless with brightness to benefit all
during your time of daylight hours,
when work we do for the wealth that's needed.
Steadfast make us, as we strive to persist
in the span we have for spending our lives —
as you do day in and day out so well.

## *Eir Prayer*

O excellent Eir, the Aesir's healer,
we praise your skills in that precious craft.
From the Hill of Healing, high in Asgard,
offer us aid and answer our prayers.
Rebuild the bodies of broken heathens;
in minds and memories, mend the fractures,
and succor the souls that have sorrow and woe.
Help us to heal our heathen families
and all the ills of our honored communities.

## *Forseti Prayer*

O famed Forseti of the flowing spring,
you still all strife with stirring counsels,
and your court is best in keeping frith.
From glorious Glitnir, give a hearing:
quell our quarrels, quickly and fairly,
with peaceful solutions that profit all.
Lead us to learn from your lawful ideal,
that we settle suits by seeking fairness
and keep our kindreds with caring frith.

## *Freyja Prayer*

O foxy Freyja, you're the famous Lady,
greatly desired by gods and etins.
Bless with beauty our bodies and souls;
let our lives flourish with lusty passion
and satisfying sex with sensuous partners.
To seekers of seið, send your guidance

in this honored art of elder times.
Let love lead us in living well,
that worthy we be of your welcome hall.

## *Freyr Prayer*

O fruitful Freyr, you're the famous Lord
who rules o'er rain and rightful sunshine.
Enchant our plows for churning the earth
as we plant our seeds for prosperous growth,
and bless our hard work with bountiful harvest.
Fuel the Folk's frith with fellowship's mead,
make strong and stable our estates in Midgard,
and help heathen hearts as they hunger for love
in finding matches for fortunate marriages.

## *Frigg Prayer*

O farseeing Frigg, Fjörgynsdóttir,
Queen of Asgard, you're quiet in sooth,
but on high Hliðskjálf, hark to our prayer:
bless the marriages and births of heathens,
and lead us to love the life that's everywhere,
but most of all, the mothers we have.
Give aid to our work of honorably weaving
the strands of our lives in the sturdy tapestries
of the healthy homes and hofs of the Folk.

## *Heimdall Prayer*

O hawk-eyed Heimdall, you're Hallinskiði
and wakeful always, the whitest of Aesir.

We praise your watch o'er worlds all nine
that is warding well the wondrous Bifröst.
In high Himinbjörg, hark to our prayer:
keep clear our sight and keen our hearing,
aid our efforts that aim for wakefulness,
make valiant our hearts for vigilant duty,
and as Ríg teach runes to our ready minds.

## *Hel Prayer*

O merciful Hel, mistress of death,
you rule that land of restful abode,
doomed to succor the dead you're sent.
The release of loved ones you allow to none,
yet hear our prayer: prepare them feasts,
make certain they gain the gifts we send,
and help them heal from their hurts in life.
Our lives with love, allow them to reach,
sending assurance of the soul's rebirth.

## *Hœnir Prayer*

O helpful Hœnir, we hail your gift,
the wode you gave to wood made human,
and the truce you sealed as tribal hostage.
Let thrive the thoughts that we think and craft
as we mold the matter of memory to gold.
Bless our brain-waves with brilliant insights
when we seek mysteries in serious matters.
Keep close to us the counsel of memory
that we ourselves can decide our ways.

## Iðunn Prayer

> O youthful Iðunn, we yearn for your apples,
> the luscious fruit that is life to the gods.
> Old age always in the end will win;
> may you stave her off, for our striving's sake
> in lust for life, as long as you can.
> Wax our vitality for work in Midgard,
> this realm of action and rightful duty,
> for our lives are short. So lift our spirits;
> make young our souls; put youth in our hearts.

## Jörð Prayer

> O holy Jörð, hallowed mother
> of mighty Thor, Midgard's champion,
> we honor you always as origin of life.
> Bless with bounties so our bodies thrive,
> and firm our footing in fimbul Midgard
> that well our work may wax with gain.
> Help us remember our commitment to you,
> that we cherish life and by choosing love,
> we keep you safe for the sibs to come.

## Kvasir Prayer

> O clever Kvasir, crafted in truce,
> we praise the peerless and potent wisdom
> that you widely shared in worlds all nine.
> Help us reconcile rigid opposites
> that we grow in wisdom and gain in the craft
> of essential synthesis as we seek inspiration.

Give talent in teaching that we travel your path
in sharing the fruits of your shining ferment,
and ward us well that this work may last.

## Landvættir Prayer

O Landvættir, you living spirits
dwelling in waters and woods and rocks,
we laud your work in warding the land.
Make fertile the fields with food aplenty,
that our tables brim with tasty delights.
Give guard to the roads for guests we welcome,
that safe and sound they seek our homes.
Bless us with aid for the offerings we bring,
and remind us well to be mindful of you.

## Máni Prayer

O main-filled Máni, you're a mighty lord
and a whirling wheel that's welcome in dark.
We praise your flight from that fiercest wolf;
may you always keep an excellent distance.
Mark and measure the months of our lives,
making us mainful as your might waxes
and lessening our woes as you wane in light.
Let rise in our souls the rune of Menon,
inspiring the learned on your lunar path.

## Mímir Prayer

O mighty Mímir, memory's warden,
we laud your head of hidden lore,

and we praise your well of potent wisdom.
Make our memories matchless and sharp
that the thoughts we think can thrive on them.
Bless our brain-waves with brilliant wisdom
that we counsel well our kindred folk.
Tell us tidings of truths unknown
that we grow in main from great mysteries.

## Njörð Prayer

O notable Njörð, Nóatún's lord,
a leader of men, lacking in malice,
your feet are the finest of the fimbul gods.
Make safe the seas when we seek to travel;
bring sprightly winds to speed our way.
Give fullness in food that we feast aplenty
and wealth in lands and worthy possessions.
Grant us the gifts that we gain such harvests
through the work we do in wisdom and pride.

## Nótt Prayer

O darkest Nótt, Nörvadóttir,
the night you bring with your needful ride,
and your rightful rhythm regulates life.
Watch o'er the world that awaits the morn,
and make safe and sound the sleep we get
during your time that's dimly lit.
Bless the delights that we best enjoy
in your restful realm; though you race away,
night after night, we know you'll return.

## Óðinn Prayer

O ominous Óðinn, you're the Aesir's lord
and galdor's father. On that gallows tree,
you gained the Runes by gifting self
to self through ordeal. We seek to grow!
Inspire our spirits to speed on your quests:
to seek the Mead, to seek the mysteries,
and ascent for our souls to seek always.
Aid our workings as we aim to join
the heroes in Valhalla, those highest of Folk!

## Sif Prayer

O sensuous Sif, celebrated goddess,
your glorious hair is the gold of dwarves
and the shining sheaves of shimmering wheat.
Make fertile those folk who are family-seeking.
Let rain make ripe the rows of crops
in the fields we tend — whether farm or office
or other realm — for an excellent harvest
to fill our tables with food and wealth,
and remind us always to remember our earth.

## Sunna Prayer

O shining Sunna, shimmering lady,
you're the light of the lands and a lovely wheel.
We praise your flight from that fiercest wolf;
may you always keep an excellent distance.
Guide our courses with your glorious light,
and keep us safe in crossing the seas,

both in outer realms and inner reaches.
Let rise in our souls the rune of Sowilo,
inspiring the seekers on your solar path.

## Thor Prayer

O thunderous Thor, our thanks we give
for your mighty defense of Midgard's Folk
by destroying the etins that would strangle life.
Your virtues we value: vigorous action,
strength, fearlessness, straightforwardness,
and a lusty appetite for life's pleasures.
Help us to grow and gain in these virtues,
that we with worth can wear your hammer
and work our wills in the world today.

## Týr Prayer

O courageous Týr, your rightful action
firmly fettered that fearsome Wolf,
saving the worlds from certain doom.
With courage fill us, and a keenest sense
of right and wrong that we reach for justice.
May we remember your mighty sacrifice
when deadly wolves endanger lives
or justice is sought by a jury's trial
or rede is against a reconciling path.

## Ull Prayer

O excellent Ull, Ýdalir's lord,
you are bold with bow and best of hunters,

a renowned warrior in worlds all nine.
Help us honor and hold our oaths,
to receive the right to swear on rings.
Assist our readiness for single combat,
that we face our foes with fiercest courage.
Gift with glory our greatest works
as a holy boon for heathen pride.

## Váli Prayer

O virtuous Váli, vengeance you got
when one night old you worked the death
of Baldur's slayer and bore him to pyre.
Inspire our spirits to speed in our duties
with unflinching zeal and fiercest courage
to honor our charges and choose what's right.
For needful redress, deal us knowledge
of ready methods and right manner
to further our honor for folk and kindred.

## Vár Prayer

O vital Vár, we value your hearing
of all our oaths, anywhere made.
Gift us honor for all we fulfill,
but punish those who are pledge-breakers.
Bless the marriages of merry heathens
and the private pacts of people together.
Remind us of vows that we venture to keep,
and grant us wisdom to wisely oath
and savvy to sense when silence is needed.

## Víðarr Prayer

O valiant Víðarr, with vital silence
we honor the space you offered at sumbel
and the space you'll save by splitting the Wolf.
Succor with silence when we seek respite
from the noisy world that gnaws at our hearts,
and nudge us to know when it's needed most,
but prepare us well for pivotal action
while we await the wisest of times
for stepping forward with striding feats.

## Eirik's Hymn

Heimdall we praise, Heaven's Warder,
and measuring Týr's might and wisdom
and Woden's works of wondrous glory —
that Eternal Drighten from time's beginning.
The worlds were shaped for shining offspring
with heaven as a roof by that Holy Ruler.
Midgard he made, Mankind's Patron,
and that Eternal Drighten truly adorned
the earth with Men for Ingvi's blessings.

# Chapter 10: Short Charms

*Waking Stave*

> This dawning day
> brings deeds of might
> for us the bold and brave.
> For gifts from the gods,
> I give my thanks;
> may I wield them well today!

*Sun Stave*

> Sunna I hail
> in Sól's bright light;
> may day bring doughty works.
> May your shining light
> give me surest might
> for all my deeds and doings.

*Washing Stave*

> May these primal waters
> make pure my life
> and wash away the ill.
> Let be borne to me
> a boon from the gods
> by washing with water today.

*Food Stave*

> For the might and main
> through this meal I gain,
> my thanks I give to the gods.
> Let their blessings bring
> to my being the strength
> that enables worthy works.

*Drink Stave*

> May this draught I drink
> drive me onward
> to honor ancestors with deeds.
> The gift of life
> they've given to me;
> may I well return their weal.

*Moon Stave*

> Mylinn I hail
> in Máni's bright light;
> may night bring needed rest.
> May your shining light
> give me surest main
> from worlds beyond awareness.

*Sleeping Stave*

> I rightly ride
> to realm of sleep,
> restoring strength in my soul.

Let the greatest tales
of gods and heroes
bring might and main through dreams.
Well will I rest,
then wake refreshed,
filled with happy health.

## *For Collecting a Blót Tine*

Hail the spirit
of this holy tree;
a gift for a gift I offer.
Take this token
for a tine of might
that I'll wield in the work of blessing.

## *For Returning a Blót Tine*

To the tree returns
this tine of might
as a circle of power is sealed.

## *For Pouring Out a Blót Bowl*

Rightly now
our rite is ended
by grounding might and main.
We pour it here
with pride and honor:
"From the gods to the earth to us,
from us to the earth to the gods
— a gift for a gift — hail!"

## *An Opening Call for Sumbel*

> Around together
> we're rightly gathered,
> and from horn we'll drink
> the heroes' draught.
> In mighty moods
> we'll mingle now
> and speak our spirits
> for a spell tonight.

## *A Closing Call for Sumbel*

> Right rounds we gave
> and rendered well;
> the working of Wyrd
> with words we shaped.
> Let's in leisure
> now lift our horns
> and merry-make
> with mirth tonight.

# Chapter 11: Other Poems

*Öfundarmál*

The towering Tree
is topped by an eagle
who scorns the serpent
for scores of slights.
Haughty, headstrong,
and highfalutin,
that proudest bird
is puffed up well.

Deep in the roots
a dragon lurks,
bitter with bile,
biting corpses.
Sour and surly
(with searing hate
for that damned eagle),
the dragon smolders.

Both up and down,
an acorner runs
along the trunk
of that lofty tree.
He whisks the words
of the wyrm and eagle
both back and forth,
those bitter insults.

Now you may hear
some nuggets of speech

that pass between
those prideful ones,
in reading here thus
the runes of the squirrel;
be wary of finding
that woe within.

*The Eagle said:*
"Scurry my squirrel,
and scamper quickly;
let that serpent slime
hear slanderous words.
Supreme I am
o'er the piddly snake
because my view
reveals all knowledge."

*The Serpent said:*
"Scurry my squirrel,
and scamper quickly;
let that 'carry-on' bird
hear accusing words.
I lord o'er realms
that lout can't see;
I simply don't value
the view he has."

*The Squirrel said:*
"The saw he said
is slander surely,
O wisest wight
of worlds all nine.
That jerk deserves
rejoinders many;

repay his gift
with a prideful 'gild."

And so it goes,
that senseless gab.
Can the hapless hawk
give help at all?
Where is the tree
of this wisdom tale?
Can Elm or Ash
offer assistance?

## Beer in Midgard

Beer, the bright drink, beautifully colored,
of malted barley and bitter hops,
is the brewer's bounty and a boon to Man.
This yeasty ferment of Yuletide cheer,
heathen feasting, and happy hours
is a much recommended and mellow drink.
Aegir has brewed his ale for the gods:
luscious lagers delightful and rich.
The best of Man barely compares,
or so we suppose. Do secretly gods
sample the draughts of simple Midgard?
In blessing bowls our beers they taste,
but know we not what name they best.
What more say I of mighty beer?
Aegir's offspring in ocean waters
are his nine daughters in the noisy sea,
the foaming waves — or frothy malt-surf
perhaps they are, the head of bubbles
in a frosty, full, and fortunate glass.

Ancient ale-runes: old poets knew them;
where might we find those magic forms?
So beer has both: a blatant side
of physical form and further beyond
an occulted side of curious lore
to seek and mix with malt's enjoyment.

## *Fyrir Íslensku Landvættirnar*

Hail the Dragon
at home in the East
who is warding Iceland well!
Swim forth now
and accept my gift,
O spirit of Iceland's awe.

Dread and defense
is the draught you give:
now let's deeply drink.
Guard me well
as I go to Iceland
to live and learn in your realm!

Hail the Eagle
at home in the North
who is warding Iceland well!
Fly forth now
and find my gift,
O spirit of Iceland's awe.

Insight and seeing
is the sip you give:
now let's deeply drink.
Inspire me well

as I speed to Iceland
to read and write in your tongue!

Hail the Bull
at home in the West
who is warding Iceland well!
Charge forth now
and achieve my gift,
O spirit of Iceland's awe.

Might and main
is the mead you give:
now let's deeply drink.
Invigorate me well
as I visit Iceland
to meet and mix with your folk!

Hail the Rock-Giant
at home in the South
who is warding Iceland well!
Stride forth now
and strive for my gift,
O spirit of Iceland's awe.

Steadfastness strong
is the stout you give:
now let's deeply drink.
Fortify me well
as I fare to Iceland
to grow and gain in your culture!

I've called to the quarters
and have come to the center
to rightly end this rite.
Forth I go now

and fare to Iceland:
hail its special spirits,
hail my journey in joy!

## Heathen Pride

We are hearty heathens,
happy and proud;
the gods of the North
we gladly hail.
The honored ancestors'
awesome gods
are kith and kin
and keep us together.

We eagerly learn
the elder lore
and the needful virtues
of noble ancestors.
Óðinn of the Aesir
we honor for wisdom,
the power of poetry,
and the potent Runes.

Týr the one-handed
— the Wolf he bound —
we honor for courage
and order in the world.
Thor we hail
for hammer of might;
he wards and hallows
our holy steads.

Freyja for freedom
and frolic we hail;
her love and pleasure
lifts our spirits.
Freyr we hail
for harvest's reward
and peace and plenty
in proper seasons.

Many more
of mighty gods
we bid and hail
in holy blessings.
In raising our horns
with holy mead,
we hail heathenry
and heathen pride!

## *New Year's Renewal*

With dark tide's passing
the dullness departs,
and the dawning day
deems a new year.
The seeds open
and seek to sprout
as new possibilities
in the naked air.

From primal chaos
its promise was made,
and right ritual
readied its gift.

Deep were the drafts
drained in its name
that gave the power
to its glorious purpose.

Needful dearly,
renewal is here;
the turning circle
continues the cycle.
So hail the New Year
for its happy time
of all potential
and ever becoming.

## *Nine Noble Virtues*

Virtues I name,
nine in all;
hallowed by heathens,
they help your life.
Noble and needful,
know them well;
prudent and powerful,
practice them well.

The first I know,
its name is Truth.
Awesome Óðinn
is always seeking it.
A path to power,
pleasure, and wisdom —
it is dear to dolts
and drightens alike.

The second I know,
its name is Self-Reliance.
If wandering the world,
your way to make,
or hallowing your home
to hold in prosperity,
have strength inside
to steer your course.

The third I know,
its name is Discipline.
Know when on the path
to peer around,
and when in the hall
to hold your tongue,
and when to act,
awesome in might.

The fourth I know,
its name is Industriousness.
Always rise early
if you aim for wealth
and mindful be
of meetly deeds,
working hard
for the hope of Jera.

The fifth I know,
its name is Perseverance.
Óðinn did hang,
eagerly on the Tree;
through nine of nights
he never quit.

Endurance obtained
the dear-bought Runes.

The sixth I know,
its name is Courage.
Hold to right
though harm may come.
Bloodthirsty Fenrir
was bound by Týr.
He lost his hand,
but hale was his soul.

The seventh I know,
its name is Fidelity.
Have fullness of faith
in friends who are true
and to ginn-holy gods
be gracious always,
choosing often
to exchange with both.

The eighth I know,
its name is Hospitality.
The self-serving ale
Aegir provided,
and his good attendants
were greatly praised;
gold in that hall
was glowing for light.

The ninth I know,
its name is Honor.
To self be true
and tread with right,

willingly keep
your words of pledge,
and in thoughts and words
and works accord.

Virtues I've named,
nine in all.
Rede they give
if rede you need.
Useful if used,
use them well,
and a hallowed name
among heathens you'll earn.

## *Perseverance*

Perseverance
is a powerful virtue.
Steadfast in struggles
you should strive to be
— resolute and firm
if facing hardship —
to succeed and prevail
in seeking victory.

Óðinn did hang
eagerly on the Tree;
through nine of nights,
he never quit;
wounded and hungry,
he willed to succeed.
Endurance obtained
the dear-bought Runes.

Óðinn went seeking
Óðrœrir's poetry;
the labor of slaves
for a long summer
had bought Bölverk
Baugi's favor.
He pilfered that mead
with patient work.

Geirröð abused
Grímnir with fire;
for eight of nights
the agony continued
'til Agnarr gave
Óðinn a drink.
Strength of commitment
had made him stay.

Gleipnir's getter
had gained for Freyr
glorious Gerð,
Gymir's daughter;
Skírnir endured,
undaunted by threats.
Tenacity fulfilled
that needful errand.

Gored upon spears,
Gullveig was burned;
that witch endured
the worst of pain
'til reborn as Heið,
bright and holy.

Unwavering purpose
won that victory.

If faced with need
and fearsome toil,
remember that Ash,
awesome in might;
though heavily oppressed,
it holds its place.
Strong you must be,
steadfast like that Tree.

## *A Valentine's Day Poem*

Is it love lurking
or just lusty thoughts
in this frigid February?
From Roman roots
is the ritual day
of venturesome valentines.

But Northern Folk
by need seek roots
amongst the gods of our garth.
To Freyja they'll turn
for finding love
or a fling to fuel their lust.

Better would be
Beltane for her,
but 'tis farther forward yet.
So don't be frigid
in this frosty month;
spark some spirited warmth.

Make hot your heart
and give hope to it,
or at least your loins this week.
Whether one night
or a wedding is sought,
Freyja will bless your bliss.

## *Wrath of Frost Giants?*

The cold has come
to the Commonwealth;
the freeze is pouring forth.
Is it focused wrath
from frost giants?
Or something else that seeps?

The North has arrived
in a needful visit,
calling her kin to awaken.
What breaks through
in the bitter cold?
Is it the awe of glorious gods?

Is Ull's essence
in the actions of winter?
In this does his being be?
Or does Skaði seek
to ski in the snow
or freedom from a spell of fever?

In the crackling cold,
give calls to the gods,
and look for the life of giants.
In its freaky physics,

find the numinous;
in the strange and odd take awe.

## *Wrath of a Tiny Etin?*

The invisible virus
is a violent etin,
the smallest of all
that smite us humans.
With fire and ice,
fever and chills,
the flesh fights back
to further life.

Was it cold or flu?
I couldn't tell.
I battled with ascorbate
and a bounty of rest.
A lingering cough
was the last of symptoms,
the final fading
of that foe's struggle.

## *A Yule Poem*

*Snow is falling,*
*silently without,*
on the ground gleaming
and giving delight.
But the Wild Hunt rides,
wending furiously,
when the cold air
whistles outside.

*Snow is falling,*
*silently without;*
the folk meanwhile
are feasting within.
The halls are decked
and the hearth blazes,
showing the spirit
of this special time.

*Snow is falling,*
*silently without;*
of sumbel and blót,
celebration begins.
The gods are fained
in this frithful stead;
the might and main
of mead is flowing.

*Snow is falling,*
*silently without;*
to gods' folk gathered,
a glad Yule comes.
With waxing light
the wheel has turned,
and holy blessings
are brought to the kin.

## *Rise and Reach the Gods!*

*O Heathen Folk*
*in hall and field,*
don't grovel to our noble gods.
The Bonds give boons

to the better heathens
as worthiness follows worth.

Óðinn is angered
by acts that are base
and empty of honor and dignity.
Frigg withholds
her favors from bullies,
the craven who shirk all chivalry.

Týr will drop
the driest tears
for folk who refuse to sacrifice.
Thor will turn
his thunderous voice
on cowards who cannot stand.

Freyja has frowns
for the feckless rabble
who lack in love for themselves.
Freyr rejects
ungenerous folk
who need but never give.

*O Heathen Folk
in hall and field,*
thank our glorious gods,
yet be worthy, wise,
and well-renowned
when you stand and strive for our gods!

Honor Óðinn,
and offer yourself
for his goals and works in the world.
Proclaim and carve

for his cult the Runes;
be worthy of his mighty mead.

Both house and home
keep whole like Frigg,
that exemplar of domestic demeanor.
With keys on your belt,
take care in your duties
for the health of kith and kin.

Trust in Týr,
and seek true selflessness;
put community over your ego.
Remember his hand
and make your sacrifices;
be worthy of the boon of the binding.

Be brave and with heart,
like boldest Thor,
and fight your battles fiercely.
With your stone steady,
stalwart and firm,
you'll be worthy of the valknut's weal.

Be forceful like Freyja
with forthright words;
have zeal for your desires and dignity.
Lead yourself
and love as you will;
be proud and independent!

Follow Freyr,
and seek frith and harvest
in all the deeds you do.
Free your friends

from the fetters that bind;
bring joy and delight to ladies.

*O Heathen Folk*
*in hall and field,*
such standing is worthy work!
But offer more,
and by aiming higher,
rise and reach the gods!

Earn the Runes
as Óðinn did:
thrive in your thirst and hunger,
ride the Tree,
and then rise again,
waxed in runic wisdom!

Spin like Frigg,
spare not your zeal,
and learn the layers of wyrd!
With wool weave
some weal-filled bonds
to improve your family's future.

Transcend yourself,
as did unswerving Týr,
for the power that binds great bale.
With a self that's serene,
reach the center,
the pole that offers order.

Through strength be holy,
like strongest Thor
who shines with self-assurance.
Seek the secrets

of his sacred hammer
to give the gift of life.

Face the flames,
as Freyja did,
and seek a bright rebirth!
From Gullveig to Heið,
she gained in power;
transform and fulfill your wyrd!

Be giving at heart,
like gladsome Freyr,
to know the finest frith
which grows the crops
and grows the kindreds;
through gifting, gain aplenty.

*O Heathen Folk
in hall and field,*
rightly stand or rise,
for the Ragnarök
is really coming,
though far in the future it seems.

Whether you stand
and strive with work
or rise and reach the gods,
on that darkest day,
there are deeds awaiting
you and the best that you bring!

But the future aside,
there's a fight today,
so aid the Aesir now!
Pride you may take

for your place in it,
but only if you stand and strive,
or only if you rise and reach!

# Index

For alphabetization, accent marks are ignored, æ is treated as "ae," œ is treated as "oe," þ is treated as "th," and ð comes after "d." Page numbers in italics indicate an entity who is referred to but not named. Words or names in parentheses provide disambiguation or indicate that the entry is a kenning or byname for someone else. Generally, the *see also* entries will point the reader to the kennings and bynames used for a particular entity.

Aegir, 44, 46, 150, 174, 192, 199. See also Fornjót's son, Hlér
Aesir, vi, xvii–xviii, 10–12, 16, 19–23, 26, 32–34, 38, 47, 58, 63, 76, 85, 92, 95–96, 102, 107, 116, 123, 135, 139, 146, 150, 161, 168–169, 174, 176–177, 195, 209. *See also* Bonds, Powers, Regin
Aesir's lord (Óðinn), 123, 148, 155, 170, 182
Agnarr, 201
Alcis, 165
Álfar, 47, 166–168. *See also* Elves
Álfheim, 56, 168. *See also* Elf-home, Ljósálfheim
Álfrigg, 13
Alsvið, 76
Althing (assembly), 163
Alvíss, 77
Amsvartnir, 12
Andhrímnir, 44
Angeyja, 60
Anglo-Saxon (meter), xvi–xvii, xx, xxiv
Angrboða, 10, 60
Annarr's daughter (Jörð), 64
Árvak, 76
Ás (one of the Aesir), 29, 67, 93, 141

Ásabrag (Thor), 139
Asgard, 9, 13, 19, 23, 32–34, 36, 38, 47, 61, 86, 91–93, 95–96, 105, 140, 146, 150, 156, 176–177
Ash (human male collective), xiv, 149, 192
Ash (Yggdrasil), 119, 147, 202
Ask, 48
Ásynja / Ásynjur (specifically-female Aesir), 54, 57, 80
Atla, 60
Atli, 141
Auð's mother (Nótt), 71
Auðumbla, 49, 52
Aurboða's daughter (Gerð), 58
Aurvandil, 27
Austri, 4
Awl, 109
Baldur, 34, 49, 55–56, 61–62, 69, 73, 79, 96, 152, 162, 174. *See also* Óðinsson
Baldur's slayer (Höð), 184
Báleyg (Óðinn), 62, 84
Barri, 28, 58
Baugi, 35–36, 110–114, 201
Beli's bane (Freyr), 154
Beowulf (hero), 162
*Beowulf* (poem), xvii
Berling, 13

Bestla, 50. *See also* Bölþorn's daughter
Bifröst, 16, 155, 178
Bilskirnir, 68, 77, 87
Björn (Thor), 108
Blóðughadda, 46
blót (blessing ritual), xxii, xxiv, 131, 188, 205
Boðn (Óðrœrir), 30
Bölverk (Óðinn), 35–36, 84, 112–115, 201
Bölverk's bounty / wine (Óðrœrir), 22, 37
Bölþorn's daughter (Bestla), 50
Bonds (Aesir), 140, 205
Borghild's son (Helgi), 61
Borr, 50, 52, 118
Bragi (god), vi, 44, 51, 63, 93, 155, 175
Bragi Boddason (skald), 162
Breiðablik (hall), 49, 69, 152
Brísingamen, 13, 15, 85, 153, 155
Brokk, 38, 51, 98, 101–109
Búri, 49, 52, 118
Byleist's brother (Loki), 15, 18
Bylgja, 46
Camp Netimus, 130–132
Commonwealth (Pennsylvania), 203
Dag, 52, 175. *See also* Delling's son
Dark-Elf home, 53, 100, 164. *See also* Dwarf-home, Svartálfheim
Delling's son / Dellingsson (Dag), 52, 175
Dísir (collective), 53, 166–167, 170–171
Dís of the Vanir (Freyja), 13
Disting, 159–160
drápa / drápur, xxi–xxiii
Draupnir, 28, 38, *51, 103–104,* 106
Dröfn, 46
Drómi, 11
dróttkvætt, xix–xxi
Dróttning of Dawn (Ostara), 160

Dúfa, 46
Dvalinn, 13
Dvergar / Dwarves (collective), xxii, 53, 145, 164
Dwarf-home / Dwarf-world, 37, 99, 101. *See also* Dark-Elf home, Svartálfheim
Dwarves' draught / drink (Óðrœrir), 39, 123
East Coast Thing, vi, xiii–xiv
Easter (Ostara), 160
Eastern lady (Ostara), 160
*Edda.* See either *Poetic Edda* or *Prose Edda*
Egill Skallagrímsson, xvi, xxi, 162
Eikþyrnir, 43
Eindriði (Thor), 24, 42, 139
Einherjar, 43–44, 54, 124–125, 169
Eir, 54, 57, 176
Eistla, 60
Eitri, 38, 51, 98, 101–105
Eldhrímnir, 44
Elf-home, 167. *See also* Álfheim, Ljósálfheim
Elf-Lord (Freyr), 166
Éljúðnir, 60
Elm (human female collective), xiv, 149, 192
Elves (collective), 93, 145, 167–168, 174. *See also* Álfar
Embla, 48
Ennilang (Thor), 27
Eternal Drighten (Óðinn), 185
etin, 1–3, 19, 21–22, 24–25, 38, 40, 42, 68, 86, 107, 111, 116, 139, 156, 176, 183, 204. *See also* giant, jötunn
Etin-home / Etin-realm, 22–23, 58, 73, 93, 110, 119. *See also* Jötunheim
Etins (collective), 24, 145
Eyrgjafa, 60
Fáfnir, 75, 160
Farbauti's son (Loki), 15, 66

Fenrir, 10, *11*, 12, 163, 199. *See also* Wolf
Fensalir, 56
Fimbultýr (Óðinn), 126, 129
Fjalar and Galar (dwarves), *59*
Fjölnir, 58, 165
Fjörgynsdóttir (Frigg), 177
flokk / flokkar, xxi–xxii
Folk (collective), 48, 59, 70, 78, 124–129, 131, 133, 159–163, 166, 168–171, 174, 177, 182–183, 202, 205–206, 208–209
Fólkvang, 55, 85
Fólkvang's lady (Freyja), 13
Fornjót's son (Aegir), 46
fornyrðislag, xv–xx, xxii–xxiii
Forseti, 49, 55, 69, 152, 176. *See also* Queller of quarrels
Frau Holle, 152–153
Freyfaxi, 163
Freyja, vi, xiv, 13–15, 19–20, 23, 33, 55, 70, 83–84, 88, 93, 118, 153, 162, 165–166, 176, 195, 202–203, 206–207, 209. *See also* Dís of the Vanir, Gefn, Gullveig, Heið, Lady, Mardöll, Sýr, Valfreyja, Vanadís
Freyr, 11, 27–28, 38, 56, 58, 70, 102–103, 105–106, 134–136, 153–154, 159, 162, 164–166, 171, 177, 195, 201, 206–207, 209. *See also* Beli's bane, Elf-Lord, Ing, Ingvi, Lord, Yngvi
Frigg, 39, 49, 56–57, 64, 154, 162, 169–170, 177, 206–208. *See also* Fjörgynsdóttir
frith, 47, 56, 58, 69, 72, 84–85, 87, 100, 112, 122, 134–136, 153–154, 157–159, 163, 166, 168, 171, 176–177, 205, 207, 209
Fulla, 57
galdor, 30, 83, 182
galdralag, xviii, xx, xxiii

Gaut (Óðinn), 30, 58, 119, 139, 171
Geats, 162
Gefjon, 57. *See also* Gylfi's opponent
Gefn (Freyja), 19
Geirröð (etin), 39–42, 58, 86, 139
Geirröð (king), 201
Gelgja, 12
Gerð, 28, 58, 135, 154, 159, 201. *See also* Aurboða's daughter, Gymir's daughter
Gersemi, 19
giant, 32, 107, 194, 203. *See also* etin, jötunn
'gild. *See* weregild
Gild. *See* Rune-Gild
Gilling's son (Suttung), 112
Gjallarhorn (for drinking), 68, 119
Gjálp (Geirröð's daughter, etin), 41, 139
Gjálp (Heimdall's mother), 60
Gjöll (bridge), 61
Gjöll (stone slab), 12
Glaðsheim, 43, 71, 125
Glasir, 45
Gleipnir, 11–12
Gleipnir's getter (Skírnir), 201
Glitnir, 55, 176
Gná, 57
Goldlocks (Sif's hair), 37, *64*, *100*, *105*, *109*
Goths, 171
Grani, 75
Greip (Geirröð's daughter, etin), 41, 139
Greip (Heimdall's mother), 60
Grérr, 13
Gríð, 40, 58, 73, 81
Gríðarvöl, 40–41, 58
Grímnir (Óðinn), 31, 201
grith, 58, 65, 77, 134
Grjóttúnagarðar, 22, 24, 27, 86
Gróa, 27
Gullfaxi, 23, 27, 68

213

Gullinbursti, 38, *51*, *103*, *106*
Gullintanni (Heimdall), 16, 155
Gulltopp, 59
Gullveig (Freyja), 85, 153, 201, 209
Gungnir, 38, *64*, *100*, 101, 105
Gunnarr, 141
Gunnlöð, 28–31, 36, 59, 73, 84, 110, 115–116, 123
Gylfi's opponent (Gefjon), 57
Gymir's daughter (Gerð), 58, 201
Hallinskiði (Heimdall), 177
Hammer of Thor (Mjöllnir), 1–3, 24–26, *51*, 68, 86, *104*, 105, 183, 195, 209
Hangatýr (Óðinn), 83
Hár (Óðinn), 16, 30, 118, 153
Harðhugað (Thor), 140
Hati, 67, *180*
*Hávamál*, xvii–xviii
Hearth of Yggdrasil (kindred), v–vi, xxii–xxiii, 122, 163–165, 168, 173
heathen, xiii–xvii, xix, xxiii, xxiv, 122, 125–126, 130–131, 133, 138, 144, 157–158, 162, 164–165, 173, 176–177, 184, 192, 195–197, 200, 205–206, 208–209
Heaven's Warder (Heimdall), 59, 154, 185
Hefring, 46
Heidnische, 152
Heið (Freyja), 85, 201, 209
Heiðrún, 43, 153
Heimdall, 16–19, 59–60, 154–155, 177, 185. *See also* Gullintanni, Hallinskiði, Heaven's Warder, Ríg, Sýr's servant, Vindlér
Hel (goddess), *10*, 60, 178
Hel (realm), 9, 61, 146, 175
Helgi, 61. *See also* Borghild's son, Hunding's bane
Hengest, 162

Hermóð, 61–62
Hild, wheel of (shield), 25
Hill of Healing, 54, 176
Himinbjörg, 59, 178
Himinglæva, 46
Hjördís's son (Sigurð), 75
Hlér (Aegir), 46, 72, 150
Hlín, 57
Hliðskjálf, 27, 177
Hlórriði (Thor), 24, 26, 45, 140
Hnitbjörg, 28, 36, 59, 113, 116
Hnoss, 19
Höð, 62, 79. *See also* Baldur's slayer
Hœnir, 31, 62, 66–67, 88–89, 93, 178
Hœnir's bud (Mímir, god), 118
hof (temple), 78, 177
Holy Ruler (Óðinn), 185
Hope (river), 12
Horsa, 162
Hrímfaxi, 71
Hringhorn, 49
Hrönn, 46
Hropt (Óðinn), 62, 83, 100, 168
Hropt's drink (Óðrœrir), 42
Hrungnir, 22–26, 45, 86, 140, 156
Hunding's bane (Helgi), 61
Hvergelmir, 5, 43, 146
Iceland, 193–195
Iðunn, xxiii, 31–33, 51, 63, 88, 91–92, *93*, 94–95, 136, 155, 162, 179
Imð, 60
Ing (Freyr), 56, 135
Ingvi (Freyr), 134, 167, 185
Inn dýri mjöðr (Óðrœrir), ii
Ívaldi's sons / Ívaldasynir, 37–38, 64, 98, 100–101
Járnsaxa, 26, 60
Jera (rune), 170–171, 198
Jólnir (Óðinn), 170
Jörð, 26, 52, 64, 71, 179. *See also* Annarr's daughter

Jörmundgand / Midgard Serpent, 10, 86
jötunn, 28. *See also* etin, giant
Jötunheim, 8, 68, 145. *See also* Etin-home
Kólga, 46
Kvasir, vi, 65, 179
Lady (Freyja), 55, 84, 134, 166–167, 176
Lærað, 43
Landvættir, 65, 180, 193
Laufey's son or issue / Laufeyson (Loki), 21, 33, 66, 102
Leyðing, 11
ljóðahátt, xvii–xviii, xx, xxii–xxiii
Ljósálfheim, 8, 145. *See also* Álfheim, Elf-home
Lóðurr, 66
Lofn, 57
*Lokasenna*, xxii
Loki, 10, 14, 16, 18–22, 31–34, 37–41, 60, 66, 88–95, 97–98, 101, 105, 107–110. *See also* Byleist's brother, Farbauti's son, Laufey's son, Lopt, Mischief's maker, Nálarson
Lopt (Loki), 21, 39, 66, 92, 94–95
Lord (Freyr), 28, 56, 134, 153, 166–167, 177
Lyngvi, 12
Magni, 26, 68, 87, 156
Man / Men (human collective), xviii, 37, 47–48, 80, 117, 120, 139–140, 146, 155, 185, 192
Mankind's Patron (Óðinn), 185
Man's friend (Thor), 42
Máni, 67, 180, 187. *See also* Mundilfari's son, Mylinn
Mardöll (Freyja), 15, 19, 85
mead (poetry in general), xix, 27, 71, 118, 124–125, 127, 129–130, 134, 136, 138, 142, 144, 149, 159, 162, 166, 171

Mead (Óðrœrir specifically), vi, xviii, 28–30, 35–37, 59, 112–113, 115–116, 126, 169, 182, 201, 207
Menon (rune), 180
Midgard, xiv, 9, 19, 37, 42, 47, 80–81, 124, 128, 139–140, 146, 156, 165, 168, 172, 177, 179, 183, 185, 192
Mím (Mímir, etin), 119
Mímir (god), 62, 67, 83. *See also* Hœnir's bud
Mímir (etin), 68, 84, 146. *See also* Mím
Mímir (both), 180
Mímisbrunn / Mímir's Well, 5, 146
Mischief's maker / Mischief (Loki), 16, 37, 66, 74, 93
Mjöllnir, 22, 26, 38, 40, 106–107, 140. *See also* Hammer of Thor
Móði, 68, 87, 156
Mökkurkálfi, 24–25
Mundilfari's son (Máni), 67
Muspellsheim / Muspell, 3, 8, 145
Mylinn (Máni), 187
Nálarson (Loki), 18
Nanna, 55, 69. *See also* Nep's daughter
Narfi's mother (Sigyn), 74
Nep's daughter (Nanna), 69
Nerthus, 69, 165
Netimus. *See* Camp Netimus
Nettie (land wight), 132–133
Níðhögg, 147, *190–191*
Niðri, 4
Níðuð, 82
Niflheim / Nifl, 3, 8, 145
Njörð, 34, 70, 76, 88, 97, 134, 154, 165, 181. *See also* Nóatún's lord
Nóatún, 76, 97
Nóatún's lord (Njörð), 34, 70, 181
Norðri, 4

215

Norns / Nornir, 70, 146–147. *See also* Urð, Verðandi, Skuld
Nörvi's daughter / Nörvadóttir (Nótt), 71, 181
Nótt, 52, 64, 71, 181. *See also* Auð's mother, Nörvi's daughter
Óðinn, vi, xiv, xvii–xviii, 9, 22–24, 29–31, 35–36, 38, 45, 49–52, 54, 56, 59, 66, 71, 73, 75, 77, 79, 81, 83, 88–89, 92–93, 96–98, 102, 104–107, 109–117, 123–127, 142–143, 155–156, 161–162, 169–170, 182, 195, 197–198, 200–201, 206, 208. *See also* Aesir's lord, Báleyg, Bölverk, Eternal Drighten, Fimbultýr, Grímnir, Hangatýr, Hár, Holy Ruler, Hropt, Jólnir, Mankind's Patron, Ölvir-Forn, Raven god, Rögnir, Sigföður, Sigtýr, Skollvald, Thund, Vegtam, Victory-Father, Woden, Worker of Wode
Óðinn's ale (Óðrœrir), 31
Óðinsson (Baldur), 174
Óðrœrir, xiv, 8, 30, 42, 59, *65*, *84*, *124*, 201. *See also* Boðn, Bölverk's bounty, Dwarves' draught, Hropt's drink, Inn dýri mjöðr, Mead, Óðinn's ale, Són, sumbel, Suttung's sumbel, Ygg's ale
*Old English Rune Poem*, xvii
Ollerus (Ull), 141
Ölvaldi's issue (Thjazi), 33, 94
Ölvir-Forn (Óðinn), 118
orlog, 151
Ostara, 160. *See also* Dróttning of Dawn, Easter, Eastern lady
Pennsylvania, 130, 132. *See also* Commonwealth
Pittsburgh, 134, 136, 165
Poconos, 130, 132
*Poetic Edda*, xiii, xv, xvii–xviii, xxii–xxiii

Powers (Aesir), 101, 174
*Prose Edda*, xiii
Queller of quarrels (Forseti), 55
Ragnarök, 12, 62, 74, 134, 209
Rán, 46, 72, 150
Ratatosk, 147, *190–191*
Rati, 36, 113
Raven god (Óðinn), 123
Ref the sly, 162
Regin (Aesir), 35, 98
Ríg (Heimdall), 59, 178
Rind, 64, 73, 79
Rögnir (Óðinn), 73
Rome, 127, 171
Rune-Gild, vi, 170
runes (general mysteries or staves), 11, 18, 28, 51, 118, 141, 159–161, 166, 175, 178, 180, 183, 191, 193
Runes (the Mysteries or Staves), xviii, 71, 83, 123–124, 126–128, 149, 161, 167, 169, 182, 195, 199–200, 207–208
runhent, xvi, xx–xxi
Rym (Thor), 25
Sæhrímnir, 44
Sága, 73
seið, 30, 55, 83, 85, 118, 153, 176
Sessrúmnir, 55
Sif, 14, 23, 37, 74, 77–78, 86, 98–99, 105, 136, 142, 182
Sigföður (Óðinn), 22
Sigmund, 44, 75, 160, 162. *See also* Völsung's son
Sigtýr (Óðinn), 67, 83, 155
Sigurð Sigmundarson, 75, 160, 162. *See also* Hjördís's son
Sigyn, 74. *See also* Narfi's mother
Sinfjötli, 44, 75, 162
Singasteinn, 16–18
Sjælland, 57
Sjöfn, 57
Skaði, 34–35, 76, 88, 95–98, 142, 203. *See also* Thjazi's daughter, Thrymheim's lady

Skaði's sire (Thjazi), 34, 95
skald / skaldic / skaldcraft, vi, xiii–xiv, 8, 36, 45, 51, 71, 84, 117–118, 123, 125, 138, 144–145, 167, 169–170, 172, 175
Skíðblaðnir, 37, 56, *64*, *100*, 101, 106
Skinfaxi, 52
Skírnir, 11, 28, 201. *See also* Gleipnir's getter
*Skírnismál*, xxii
Sköll, 76, *182*
Skollvald (Óðinn), 119
Skuld, 70, 147. *See also* Norns
Sleipnir, 22–23, 61, 66, 71, 75
Snotra, 57
Sökkvabekk, 73
Sól (Sunna), 186
Són (Óðrœrir), 30
Sönnung (Thor), 26, 41
Sowilo (rune), 183
Steed (Yggdrasil), 148
Suðri, 4
Suebi, 82
sumbel (drinking ritual), xiv, xviii, xxii–xxiii, 73, 173, 185, 189, 205
sumbel (Óðrœrir), 29, 112–113, 117
Sunna, 67, 76, 136, 156, 161, 182, 186. *See also* Sól
Surt, 147
Suttung, 28–29, 36, 59, 110–113, 116. *See also* Gilling's son
Suttung's sumbel / mead (Óðrœrir), 112, 123
Svaðilfari, 20, *21*, 22
Svartálfheim, 8, 145. *See also* Dark-Elf home, Dwarf-home
Sweden, 57
Swedes, 165
Sýn, 57
Sýr (Freyja), 17
Sýr's servant (Heimdall), 17
Thing (assembly), 78, 138, 163

Thjálfi, 25–26
Thjazi (and as eagle), *32*, 33–35, 88, *89–91*, 92, 94, *95*, 96–97. *See also* Ölvaldi's issue, Skaði's sire
Thjazi's daughter (Skaði), 35, 76, 98
Thjóðólfr Arnórsson, xxi
Thor, vi, xiv, xxii–xxiii, 2–3, 22–27, 37–42, 58, 64, 66, 68, 74, 77, 86, 98–99, 102, 105–106, 108, 139, 141, 156, 162, 164, 179, 183, 195, 206–208. *See also* Ásabrag, Björn, Eindriði, Ennilang, Harðhugað, Hlórriði, Man's friend, Rym, Sönnung, Véurr, Vingþórr
Thrúð, 74, 77, 87
Thrym, 86, 156
Thrymheim, 92, 94
Thrymheim's lady (Skaði), 76
*Thrymskviða*, xv
Thund (Óðinn), 148
Thviti, 12
Tooth-Gnasher, 87
Tooth-Grinder, 87
Tree (Yggdrasil) 43, 71, 83, 121, 123, 145–150, 161, 182, 190, 198, 200, 202, 208
Týr, 10, 12, 78, 82, 157, 162–164, 183, 185, 195, 199, 206–208
Uð, 46
Ulfrún, 60
Ull, 17, 74, 78, 141–142, 157, 183, 203. *See also* Ollerus, Wuldor, Wulþuz, Ýdalir's lord
Uppi, 4
Urð, 70, 147. *See also* Norns
Urðarbrunn / Urð's Well, 6, 146–147
*Vafþrúðnismál*, xvii
Valfreyja (Freyja), 85
Valgrind, 43
Valhalla / Valhöll, 19, 42, 45, 61, 75, 77, 124, 169, 182

Váli, 73, 79, 184
valknut, 207
Valkyrjur / Valkyries (collective), 44, 54, 79
Vanadís (Freyja), 84, 153, 166
Vanaheim, 8, 80, 145
Vanir, vi, 80, 84, 135, 145, 165. *See also* Wanes
Vár, 57, 80, 184
Vartari, 109
Vé, 50, 81
Vegtam (Óðinn), 44, 79
Verðandi, 70, 147. *See also* Norns
Vestri, 4
Véurr (Thor), 25, 42, 140
Victory-Father (Óðinn), 44
Víðarr, vi, 16, 58, 81, 185
Viði, 81
Vili, 50, 81
Vimur, 40
Vindlér (Heimdall), 17
Vingþórr (Thor), 27
Völsung, 162
Völsung's son (Sigmund), 75
Völund, 82
völur (seeresses), 159
*Völuspá*, xv
Vör, 57
Wanes (Vanir), 165–166
Well (of Wyrd), 70, 121, 127, 148, 151
weregild / 'gild, 12, 28, 34, 76, 96–97, 107, 192

wights, xiv, xxii, 1–7, 9, 72, 131–133, 158, 191
Wild Hunt, 143, 204
wode, 8, 54, 62, 84, 120, 123, 125, 145, 167, 178
Woden (Óðinn), 118, 185
Wolf (Fenrir), 78, 81, 157, 163, 183, 185, 195
Wood (Yggdrasil), xvi, 63, 146, 148
Worker of Wode (Óðinn), 148
World-Tree (Yggdrasil), 70, 122, 173
Wuldor (Ull), 141
Wulþuz (Ull), 141
wyrd (general force), 79, 83, 146, 152, 167–171, 208–209
Wyrd (quasi-deity), 5–6, 125, 189
Ýdalir, 141
Ýdalir's lord (Ull), 78, 183
Yew (Yggdrasil), 68
Ynglings, 165–166
Yngvi (Freyr), 165
Ygg's ale (Óðrœrir), 10, 19, 145
Yggdrasil, 121, 145, 149, 161. *See also* Ash, Steed, Tree, Wood, World-Tree, Yew
Ymir, 49–50, 81
Yule / Yuletide, 144, 169–170, 192, 205
Zisa, 82

www.ingramcontent.com/pod-product-compliance
Lightning Source LLC
Chambersburg PA
CBHW021433080526
44588CB00009B/517